D0873266

VISIONS OF REALITY

What Fundamentalist Schools Teach

VISIONS OF REALITY

What Fundamentalist Schools Teach

Albert J. Menendez

PROMETHEUS BOOKS
Buffalo, New York

For Shirley

Published 1993 by Prometheus Books

97 96 95 94 93   5 4 3 2 1

Library of Congress Cataloging-in-Publication Data

Menendez, Albert J.
    Visions of reality : what fundamentalist schools teach / by Albert J. Menendez.
        p.   cm.
    Includes bibliographical references.
    ISBN 0-87975-802-3
    1. Fundamentalist churches—Education—United States.   I. Title.
LC586.F85M46   1992   92-33260
377′.8′0973—dc20   CIP

Published in cooperation with Americans for Religious Liberty, P.O. Box 6656, Silver Spring, Maryland 20916. Americans for Religious Liberty (ARL) is a nonprofit public interest educational organization, founded in 1981, dedicated to preserving the American tradition of religious, intellectual, and personal freedom in a pluralistic secular democratic state. Membership is open to all who share that purpose. ARL publishes a newsletter and other material, operates a speakers bureau, and has been involved in litigation in defense of separation of church and state and freedom of conscience. Inquiries are welcomed.

Printed in the United States of America on acid-free paper.

TABLE OF CONTENTS

INTRODUCTION:

RELIGIOUS BIGOTRY AND PUBLIC POLICY

This book is based on a careful, analysis of sixteen major textbooks published by fundamentalist Christian publishers for the private school and home schooling markets. These texts, totaling 8,793 pages of material, are devoted to American history, world history, U.S. government, geography, American literature, British literature, and the natural sciences.

These books were issued in the 1980s and 1990s by the two leading fundamentalist Protestant publishing houses, which began to service the fast-growing private school constituency in the mid-1970s.

The textbooks selected for analysis in this study represent the fundamentalist wing of Protestant Christianity and are used in schools which reflect this orientation. They may be and usually are "nondenominational" but they may also be connected with individual churches, congregations, or denominations, often those of independent Baptist groups.

These texts never define fundamentalism, other than to suggest that it is the only true version of the Christian religion.

A typical expression of this certitude can be seen in a passage from a modern British literature text which claims: "Today vital Christianity on any considerable scale can be found only among the Free Presbyterian churches of Northern Ireland."[1] This information will surely come as a surprise to the 99% of other Christians in the United Kingdom who do not belong to the Reverend Ian Paisley's sect.

A reasonable definition would be that fundamentalism is a movement, originating in the late nineteenth and early twentieth centuries, that emphasizes the infallibility and inerrancy of the Bible as the only rule of faith and authority in human life, that requires a personal born-again religious experience, and that emphasizes personal evangelism to convert humanity. It tends to reject the historical development of Christianity since the Apostolic era and rejects the mediatorial role of the institutional church. The fundamentalist "temper" exists in all religions and is often regarded as close-minded and intolerant of other positions. There are today thriving fundamentalist movements in Islam, Roman Catholicism, and Judaism as well as in Protestantism. The term as used in the United States refers almost always to Protestantism, and the use of the term often clarifies political and educational debates.

This definition is by no means complete. Evangelical Protestant Christianity is closely related to fundamentalism, and shares many of its presuppositions. But evangelicals do not like, as a general rule, the implications of separatism and intolerance toward others which modern fundamentalism implies. There are many evangelically-oriented church schools, in the Mennonite, Reformed and Lutheran traditions especially, which would be appalled by the approach to education which will be revealed in this analysis.

It should be noted that not all of the attitudes or emphases revealed in this analysis constitute bigotry or prejudice. Nor will only fundamentalists agree with them. What this analysis suggests, however, is that these textbooks and by extension the schools using them present only very one-sided views of history, geography, literature, and science. Furthermore, students are not encouraged to examine issues or to seek for answers to complex questions themselves. They are actively discouraged from doing so. The selection of material and the interpretations given foreclose any independent analysis and seem intent on creating a generation of adults with a mindset that can only be harmful to democratic freedoms and to interfaith harmony.

It cannot be stressed too often that these textbooks are designed for secular areas of study. No analysis has been included for religion, theology, or Bible course studies, which would have been inappropriate since schools operated by certain religious groups for essentially religious purposes would be expected to impart a defense of their own religious beliefs and concerns. What was perhaps not expected was the degree to which religious conviction shaped historical, scientific, and literary conclusions, and created an educational world totally unlike that of any other.

The first two chapters in this book reveal the critical attitude held by these textbooks toward all other world religions, including other expressions of Christianity. Since the authors of these texts seem preoccupied with the Roman Catholic Church, its history and people, a separate chapter has been devoted to the intense and wholly critical attention accorded to the subject.

The third chapter describes the right wing political bias which is characteristic of these books. The treatment of literature is the subject of the fourth chapter, and it is followed by a discussion of how these books present scientific, ecological and environmental concerns. The concluding chapter looks at certain historical questions which receive biased and questionable treatment in these texts.

As this study will soon make painfully clear, the views and attitudes expressed are sharply at variance with the major tenets of American democracy: respect for diversity, intellectual freedom, maximum choice in lifestyle, religious tolerance, racial and cultural pluralism, appreciation for modernity, experimentation, and pragmatism. All of these values are denied. Most are ridiculed. The fundamental concepts of the American democratic experiment for two centuries are denounced repeatedly. Religious bigotry and a contempt for non-fundamentalist Protestant perspectives and viewpoints permeate these supposedly secular subject textbooks.

Students who receive their entire educational experience in schools which use these books will absorb visions of reality that are abhorrent to the vast majority of Americans, especially to those whose religious faiths are slandered and distorted.

These books promote intolerance, separatism, and political reaction. They idealize an American past that itself was intolerant and unjust or, in some cases, simply imaginary. The kind of government preferred by these authors is a theocracy, or at best a very limited democracy which restrains various activities considered immoral and represses the cultural and religious values of those who are not conservative Protestants. Catholics, religious liberals, and moderate-to-liberal Protestants are seen as enemies, not as fellow citizens and passengers on the planet of life. These texts clearly prefer the American colonies, not the nation which banned religious establishments, religious tests for public office, and mandated separation of church and state. They wax eloquent over Puritan autocracy and the various forms of single or multiple Protestant establishments of the eighteenth century. They show no appreciation for religious or ethnic pluralism. In short, these texts create a permanent ghetto of the mind for their students.

It must, however, be clearly acknowledged that these schools have a constitutional right to exist. (The *Pierce* case in 1925 settled that issue.) These textbooks and their writers have every right to co-exist with other viewpoints in the great marketplace of ideas that characterizes this country.

These biases apparently reflect the prejudices of those who manage and support these schools. The intense anti-Catholicism of these texts clearly reflects the prevailing attitudes of fundamentalism today. Here are two examples. The Reverend Tim LaHaye, a fundamentalist Baptist firebrand, ordered the firing of two Catholic teachers from his Christian High School in El Cajon, California, in 1981. His actions were based solely on the teachers' religious affiliation, not their professional record.[2] In Texas the Longview Christian Academy canceled a basketball game with another school after years of competition when school officials discovered their opponents were Catholics.[3] Paul F. Parsons, in his groundbreaking study, *Inside America's Christian Schools*, found that fundamentalist schools "consider Catholicism to be a form of fraudulent Christianity and abhor a variety of Catholic practices and beliefs."[4]

Parsons also found that these schools "have a tendency to emphasize rote learning and to downplay the importance of free thought,"[5] "want doctrinal instruction to accompany history lessons,"[6] and frequently engage in "a strictness that borders on repressiveness."[7]

Alan Peshkin's study also concluded that these schools promote a unitary and all-encompassing worldview and are "total institutions, the natural organizational outcome of schools based on absolute truth."[8]

There is a public policy issue. Many of these schools and their advocates and patrons are now seeking public funding on both the state and federal levels. In concert with other private and religious schools, they are mounting political pressure so that all American taxpayers will be compelled, under various specious choice and voucher schemes, to subsidize the world-views promoted.

It is no surprise that Republican members of Congress, and a Republican President, who will ultimately benefit from voters indoctrinated by these books, are the primary advocates of public support for sectarian private schools. The Bush Administration's voucher proposal, which would lead to substantial public funding of private and parochial schools, was defeated in January in the United States Senate by a 57 to 36 vote. Not surprisingly, 33 of 39 Republican Senators favored the proposal while 51 of 54 Democrats opposed it.

This brings us to the core of the problem. These schools, which are attended by well over one million students, could be eligible for substantial public funding if the Bush Administration and its allies in Congress have their way. So-called voucher and "choice" programs are being promoted as ways to improve the nation's admittedly problem-plagued education. These schemes, instead of helping the public schools which educate 89% of American students, would divert federal funding to private schools, most of which exist for religious reasons and are operated by religious bodies. Not all church schools engage in religious bigotry but nearly all of them discriminate in faculty hiring and admissions policies. None are under meaningful public control. It has been a longstanding principle in American life that the public should have significant control over those institutions which it funds. Neither should anyone be compelled to pay taxes for the promotion of a religion with which he or she disagrees.

No public funds—on the federal or state levels—should be given to schools which inculcate religious prejudice. Nor should religiously-biased textbooks be given or loaned to these schools. (Seventeen states allow this practice, at present, though it is uncertain how many provide the previously described textbooks.)

The increasing fragmentation and disharmony in American society can only be exacerbated if publicly-funded enclaves of sectarian bigotry become more widespread. *Caveat emptor.*

NOTES

1. Ronald A. Horton, *British Literature for Christian Schools: The Modern Tradition, 1688 to the Present* (Greenville, SC: Bob Jones University Press, 1982), p. 359.

2. *Los Angeles Times*, April 30, 1981, p. 1.

3. *Arkansas Gazette*, December 31, 1983, p. 5.

4. Paul F. Parsons, *Inside America's Christian Schools*, (Macon, GA: Mercer University Press, 1987), p. 137.

5. *Ibid.*, p. 174.

6. *Ibid.*, p. 171.

7. *Ibid.*, p. 135.

8. Alan Peshkin, *God's Choice: The Total World of a Fundamentalist Christian School* (Chicago: University of Chicago Press, 1986), p. 258.

1

HERETICS, ALL

Attacks on the religious beliefs and positions of those who do not adhere to Fundamentalist Protestant Christianity are pervasive in the history, geography, civics, literature, and even science texts examined in this study. Students are repeatedly warned that Americans "were led astray by various perversions of Christianity"[1] and that "Usually in the guise of being Christian, new movements arose which denied the absolute authority of Scripture. . ."[2] A literature text says, "Religions such as these deny the Christian doctrines necessary for salvation but still claim to give inner peace and a purpose for living."[3]

The existence of alternative religious groups is anathema to fundamentalists because "false teachings have always been part of history."[4] The newly-established and American-born religions like Christian Science, Seventh-day Adventism and the Jehovah's Witnesses are labeled "newly organized cults that denied Biblical truths."[5] These "cults offered attractive ideas to religious Americans and won great followings, but they also blinded people to the truths of God's Word."[6]

A literature text argues that individualism produced evil religions. "This emphasis on individualism also influenced religious thought. During the reign of romanticism, cults like

Mormonism and Seventh-Day Adventism emerged. In such cults, the teaching of an individual is elevated over the truth of the revealed Word of God."[7]

Another text reiterates this theme. "The false teachings of cults are Satanic counterfeits of true Biblical Christianity, and many people are easily deceived by them. Whenever a broad-scale revival of Biblical Christianity takes place, Satan raises up his counterfeits to draw people away from the truth of God's Word. In the northeastern section of the United States, where the revivals of the early nineteenth century had a great impact, Satan raised up three major cults in less than two decades."[8] Christian Science is also called "a deluding and dangerous cult."[9]

Attacks of this severity on other Christians can only be calculated to create religious prejudice and fear.

RELIGIOUS LIBERALS

Religious liberals and supporters of the social gospel are roundly condemned. "Religious liberalism began to undermine the American tradition and helped to give rise to new humanistic philosophies."[10] Furthermore, "The social gospelers often addressed real social issues, but they came to rely upon mere legislation rather than upon the proclamation and the application of the gospel of Christ as the solution to all social ills."[11] The "Modernists," who tried to reconcile religious dogmatism with scientific and philosophical inquiry, are said to have "denied all of the fundamentals of the historic Christian faith."[12] Not some Christian doctrines, but *all* of them! Those who tried to bring about greater understanding between different Christian traditions are ridiculed. "One of the chief thrusts of the Modernists was a false ecumenism, or outward union of all churches and sects into one organization regardless of creedal and doctrinal differences."[13]

An American literature text unloads a barrage of criticism on religious liberalism. "By trying to make the Bible agree with erroneous scientific theories, they denied the essential truths of Christianity."[14]

The usual siege mentality conveyed in the Bob Jones University textbook series is reaffirmed. True Christians are always a minority, battling for truth in an unbelieving world. "Liberalism came to dominate the seminaries, the most prominent churches, the Sunday school materials, and the religious press."[15] Liberals, we are told, "gave easy, psychological solutions to the universal problem of sin."[16] Those who supported the social gospel "departed from God's Word."[17]

Liberal Protestantism "has steadily undermined the nation's religious inheritance"[18] because it "attempts to accommodate traditional Christianity to a godless, modern view of the world. In fact, it deliberately elevates man's mind over God's. For whenever a conflict arises between the modern mind and the Bible, the Bible in liberal thinking, always bows to the modern mind."[19] Harry Emerson Fosdick's writing is called "false teaching."[20] In summary, "All these false versions of true religion and worship contribute to the growing theological anarchy of a nation whose people do merely what seems right in their own eyes."[21]

An American literature text proclaims, "Religious liberalism is only a modern form of the paganism of Christ's day."[22]

In a civics text we read, "Religious liberalism . . . hardened many Americans in their sin."[23] Many missionaries, "lacking a personal knowledge of Christ as Savior themselves, spread a 'social gospel' which stressed the good works of humanitarian aid rather than salvation through Jesus Christ."[24] "The preachers of the social gospel . . . have not recognized their own sin and need of Christ, and they expect their good works of humanitarianism to satisfy God,"[25] we are informed.

This contempt for humanitarianism and "good works" permeates the text. This bias cannot help but predispose students toward indifference concerning the physical needs of the distressed.

Religious liberals are also blamed for moral decline. "As German rationalists and other theologians cast doubts on the truth of Scripture, their ideas began to break down the standards of many religious groups in America."[26]

Deists have "an un-Biblical view of God,"[27] and one of their primary spokespersons, Thomas Jefferson, is criticized for compiling his own edition of the Bible. "Jefferson's shortened gospels show us that we cannot expect the natural man—then or now—to receive the things of the Spirit of Christ . . . "[28] Furthermore, Jefferson's belief in immortality is ascribed to personal sorrow. "Jefferson did believe in a vague personal immortality. Perhaps that was because his wife and child had preceded him in death. . ."[29]

Christians who are concerned about social justice and alleviating the conditions of the poor are constantly reviled. Around 1900, "Churches were accepting liberal doctrine and placing less emphasis on the authority of the Bible than on doing social good."[30] Elaborating on this, the text says, "Beginning in the 1800s, many liberal 'Christians' became convinced that their mission was to reform society by removing its evils and 'Christianizing' the world. This concept became known as the social gospel. The social gospel was truly 'another gospel' (Galatians 1:6), since it held that salvation comes to the person who does good works for mankind. Proponents of the social gospel viewed man as basically good and constantly improving."[31] The Federal Council of Churches "was founded for the purpose of promoting social reforms through religion. Rather than reaching individual men through the biblical gospel, the FCC sought to 'redeem' all of society, making men good by eliminating all social evils. . . .Many members of the FCC were genuine Christians who were simply side tracked from the primary purpose of the church. Others, however, did not even pretend to believe the Bible."[32]

World War I "thoroughly discredited" the hopes of religious liberals.[33] America's "religious leaders, many of whom had long rejected biblical authority, were of little help."[34]

UNITARIANS

Unitarianism is portrayed as a uniquely evil and highly influential religion. It "deceived many, especially among the influential in education and politics."[35] Indeed, the rise of Unitarianism is seen as evidence of "the extent of the religious decline of America."[36]

Unitarianism is labeled a "false religion" which "ignored man's need for forgiveness of sin through the blood of Christ and said that men should simply follow the teachings of Jesus and the dictates of their own reason."[37]

Unitarians are called "an unbelieving religion"[38] and "an unBiblical philosophy."[39] Some Americans "allowed Unitarianism to destroy their faith in Jesus Christ and God's Word."[40] Elsewhere, students are told: "Although Unitarians claimed to believe the Bible, they denied man's need of salvation through the blood of Christ."[41] In a sarcastic passage asking students, "Why do you suppose Unitarianism could take over churches that once believed the Bible?"[42] the teacher is told to respond, "The people were probably ignorant of the Bible's teachings, and they did not recognize that their schools and pastors were teaching ideas contrary to the Word of God."[43]

Unitarians are linked to other evil liberals of today in this passage. "Notice that Unitarianism gained control of Harvard. When un-Scriptural beliefs take hold in the colleges and seminaries that train preachers, the schools pass those un-Scriptural beliefs to the pastors they are sending out to churches. The pastors take the errors they were taught and pass them on to their people in the churches, and those churches fall away from the faith. This same pattern has been followed in many Protestant denominations that once taught the inerrancy of the Bible. Liberal teachers in denominational schools began to question the authority of Scripture, and the pastors they trained went out to destroy the faith of the people in their churches."[44] The authors return to this theme later, adding that, "The faith of many Americans was being eroded by unbelieving preachers, even in that day. As the years passed, more and more people followed the teachings of such men instead of supporting the preachers who continued to stand for the truth of God's Word."[45] In short, Unitarianism was "a movement that denied many truths of the Christian faith."[46]

HUMANISTS

The Humanist perspective on life may be a growing and increasingly admired alternative to many people in the United States and Western Europe but it is seen as an abomination by conservative Protestants.

In a brand-new American literature text, the author informs his students that "Secular humanism is, in fact, a substitute religion, glorifying the creation rather than the Creator. Many developments in American education and society are directly traceable to the influence of this movement. . ."[47] Secular humanism, which "has tried to replace God with man,"[48] controls U.S. life today. In unmistakable terms, we are informed, "This secular faith of the humanists has greatly affected modern thought. Their faith underlies the actions of social engineers in the federal government seeking to control American life and make a unified society. It prevails in the thoughts of most writers and other national spokesmen, especially those of the public media. It permeates the nation's textbooks and educational philosophy. . ."[49]

In addition, the Humanist Manifesto "flaunts its rejection of the Bible and its foolish faith in man's ability to create a new world."[50]

In another American history text we read, "Humanism is an overemphasis on human worth and ability, leading man to glorify himself instead of God. . . . While its historical forms may vary, humanism inevitably leads people away from God and spiritual concerns. It promotes the false idea that man is good and that he is superior to God. Secular humanism of the twentieth century altogether rejects belief in God and worships man as God. The pride of humanism, however, will not go unpunished. . ."[51]

This same text says that "Common to all foes of Christianity was a spirit of humanism—the exaltation of man above God."[52]

In an American history text, secular humanism is defined as a "man-made religion which replaces the divine Creator with evolution, heaven with hopes of a man-made utopia, Christ with human leaders, sin with social deviance, biblical doctrine with human knowledge, and the gospel with social reform."[53]

In a biology textbook, we are informed that "Anyone who is a humanist is a practical believer in Scientism, the worship of science."[54]

An American literature text really gets carried away. Every human evil is subsumed under the humanist mantle. We are told, "Every false idea of the [20th] century can be regarded as a form of humanism—a conscious elevation of man above God brought on by a conscious revolt against the authority of the Bible, God's Word."[55]

Thus, humanism is seen as the summation of all evils and errors in the human experience, "the worship of man" and "the old pagan ideas of pantheism"[56] rolled into one.

Humanism is blamed for the decline of public schools during the 1950s and 1960s. "The secularization of the public schools during the preceding decade had contributed to the cultural revolution of the sixties. Public schools had taught humanistic philosophy with its permissiveness and its theory of evolution, thus reducing man to the level of an animal and giving him no purpose for life."[57] The humanist view of life is condemned for creating a corrupt society during the 1970s. "The humanistic principles of man's autonomy and 'do your own thing' had permeated every aspect of the culture. The American society of the seventies adopted a defiant attitude that touched old and young alike—if a person was not satisfied with events, he would strike, riot, or vocally protest. Throughout the sixties and into the seventies, new groups were constantly forming, each clamorously proclaiming their rights.   The Constitutional guarantee of freedom of speech was being abused by a spoiled, selfish society."[58]

This depiction of Humanism and humanist values is hardly objective or intended to inform students.   It is a crude caricature designed to create hatred and fear in the readers.

MORMONS

The Mormons are seen as "one of several cults, or false religions." [59] Mormonism's founder, Joseph Smith, "claimed to have used magic spectacles to translate some Egyptian writing on golden plates; the plates conveniently disappeared before anyone but Smith and a few friends could see them. Salvation, according to Mormon doctrine, rests solely upon good works. One who is good enough eventually becomes a god, equal to the God of the Bible. . . . Because of their polygamy and other unusual practices, Mormons were harassed at their thriving settlement at Nauvoo, Illinois."[60]   It is said that Smith was "killed by a mob made up of both non-Mormons and Mormons who opposed him."[61]

In another text Mormons are described in this way: "Mormonism is a cult, a religious group that denies at least one major doctrine of the faith and holds to some extreme religious positions outside of historic Christianity. According to Mormon doctrine, salvation rests solely on good works. Mormons even believe that they can become gods, equal to the God of the Bible, if they are good enough."[62] They are also said to teach "false doctrines."[63]

QUAKERS

Pennsylvania's Quaker founders are ridiculed in a way that diminishes the respect that students might otherwise have felt for them. "While the sincerity of the Quakers was admirable, their religious viewpoint was unbiblical. Their basic error was their belief that man could be led by an 'inner light,' independent of the teachings of God's Word, and that man's good works and disciplined life would gain him eternal reward."[64]

Rhode Island's Quakers are criticized.   "During the seventeenth century many Quakers, sincere and zealous, apparently believed the gospel and honored the Bible. But there were dangerous tendencies of the Quaker belief. Most Quakers tended to rely more strongly for truth and guidance on an 'inner light'—the internal leading of what they claimed was the Holy Spirit—than on the Bible. . . .During the late seventeenth century they also tended to emphasize personal conduct (good works) more than a personal relationship with God."[65]

Once again, Penn's colony is criticized on religious grounds. "The Quakers, despite their unbiblical reliance upon emotions, founded well-ordered and prosperous towns. They held many biblical beliefs and made many positive contributions to our history. But precisely because their beliefs were so close to gospel truth, they were dangerous to biblical Christianity. Their error of adding human revelation to God's Word caused many to be led into spiritual darkness."[66]

GREEK ORTHODOX

Greek Orthodox Christianity is ridiculed in several passages from a world history textbook. "Although the Orthodox church claims to teach correct doctrine, many of her beliefs are contrary to Scripture."[67] Both the Roman and Orthodox churches are ridiculed for "adoption of nonbiblical elements."[68] An informative discussion of icons is also slanted. "Religious art in itself is not wrong, but the Orthodox have virtually turned their icons into objects of worship by kissing them and burning incense before them."[69]

Disdain for the Orthodox Church continues unabated. The conversion of Russian ruler Vladimir to the Orthodox faith is ridiculed. It is explained that the king "rejected Roman

Catholicism because the Catholic churches were dark and damp and the services were dull"[70] but the Orthodox liturgy is described as "gorgeous" and "beautiful." The event is then twisted to allow the author to indulge in an irrelevant homily. "Today many people are just like Vladimir. They choose a religion that makes them comfortable or that appeals to their intellect. . . . Since Christ does not promise His followers a life of ease and pleasure, the unconverted world wants nothing to do with biblical Christianity. But those who know Christ as Saviour would not exchange the riches of their faith for all the manmade religions the world has to offer."[71]

EPISCOPALIANS AND ANGLICANS

Anglicans and Episcopalians are repeatedly denounced as effete, corrupt and much too Catholic in these fundamentalist school texts. Ronald Horton's text on modern British literature sets the tone when he says the Anglican Church is "dead in ritualism and rationalism and serves mainly a ceremonial function."[72]

This bias against Anglican Christianity permeates another modern English literature text. The Church of England is accused of betraying the people. "The church in England in the eighteenth century was formal, cold, and dead. It was the fashion to attend church, but the impersonal God of deism could do nothing to change the hearts and daily lives of the people. The Anglican Church was hopelessly entangled in politics, and many priests were in the church only because of the living it provided. The highest church leaders were often worldly and unfit for their positions. One archbishop, Cornwallis, had to be reprimanded by the king for his wild parties."[73] This passage is typical of the texts used in fundamentalist schools. They exaggerate the extent of religious decline and apostasy within Roman Catholic and Anglican societies in order to justify the necessity of the Protestant Reformation and the evangelical, Methodist and nonconformist movements in England. They ignore the extent of reformist activity within the Roman and Anglican communions and completely ignore the movements of spiritual reform and revitalization which produced the Counter Reformation and the Oxford Movement.   This is a highly questionable approach, an example of historical writing which seeks to shape historical facts to justify religious propaganda. The text proclaims, for example: "At such a wicked and desperate time in English history, God raised up spiritual leaders whose preaching and writing reached thousands, turning England back to the God of the Bible."[74]

Jonathan Swift's writings are considered "unwholesome and mockingly pessimistic."[75]   This is somehow related to his being an Anglican clergyman, as we are informed in this passage: "That Swift was an Anglican minister illustrates something about the state of the clergy and the church in the first half of the eighteenth century."[76]   Furthermore, Swift "made fun" of evangelical preachers, "appeared to be more concerned about the material and political than the spiritual well-being of his parishioners" and "was reported to have used church funds for trips to London to promote his literary works."[77]   Then, "His mind failed about three years before his death,"[78]   So much for one of the greatest satirists in the English language.

Religious bias shapes the commentary section on the devotional writers.   About George Whitefield students are reminded, "It was God's power in his life that made him successful."[79]   A Whitefield quote on the Bible is pointedly used as a referent.   "'I got more true knowledge from reading the book of God in one month than I could ever have acquired from all the writings of men.'"[80]   The Anglican Church is ridiculed once again: "Because the established church disliked evangelistic messages and closed the churches to him, he began preaching outdoors."[81]   In Whitefield's journal selection, however, he refers to fasting and receiving the "Sacrament of the Holy Eucharist."[82]   Obviously, he did not reject the Church of England's devotional life.   In a later section the six evangelical Protestant writers of the Victorian era are given much more favorable treatment than the five Anglican or Anglo-Catholic writers. Of the brilliant John Mason Neale we are told, "His pro-Catholic leanings alienated him from many of the churchmen of his day. . ."[83] (The authors also can't quite decide whether Anglican clergy are called pastors, ministers, or priests. All three terms appear on page 375, which must be confusing to the students.)

In a discussion of "hymn writers of the Romantic Age," the author's prejudices against Anglican Christianity are intrusive. Thomas Kelley, it is said, "was converted while studying law at Trinity College in Dublin and decided to become an Anglican minister."[84] But, "His strong evangelistic preaching and insistence on the doctrine of justification by faith brought him into conflict with Anglican officials, and he became an independent minister."[85] Henry Francis Lyte "became an Anglican minister, but was evidently not saved until later."[86]

A U. S. history text portrays Anglican settlers in a highly unfavorable light.

Anglicans first appear in a section on the Separatists, who, we are told, "wanted to be free to worship and live as the Scriptures taught. Because their scriptural beliefs often caused them to disagree with the teachings of the established Anglican church, they were harassed and persecuted."[87] The Anglican Church "was primarily a political organization under Elizabeth I, and although the church was usually tolerant, it was intolerant of the Separatists, who emphasized the authority of the Bible rather than that of the church."[88]

The Puritans are praised for "sacrificing many things to come and establish a Bible-honoring community. . . .All had been harassed, ridiculed, and generally abused for wanting to see scriptural authority restored in the Church of England."[89] Episcopalians would say that scriptural authority had never been lost in their church, so it did not have to be restored.

Attempts to describe Anglicanism fall short of accuracy. "Those who supported formalism and ritual were called High Church Anglicans; those who favored strong biblical preaching and were less interested in ritual were known as Low Church Anglicans. Most of the Anglican settlers at Jamestown were Low Church."[90] As a matter of fact, High Anglicans emphasized apostolic succession, Eucharistic worship and sacramental religion. Ritual and liturgy were not the central concerns of the High Anglicans under Archbishop Laud, the Caroline Divines, or the Oxford movement.

Criticism continues. "The quality of both the Anglican ministers and their churches deteriorated by the end of the seventeenth century."[91] "The Anglican church remained the strongest church in Virginia, however, and opposed others, sometimes fiercely, until after the formation of the United States."[92] Anglican priests are continually referred to as ministers or even as preachers,[93] another inaccuracy.

The text also claims, "The Anglican churches in the Carolinas generally lacked the biblical emphasis of some of the other Protestant churches."[94]

In a section on immorality in the colonial clergy, an Anglican "minister" in Philadelphia, a "Parson Phillips" is singled out as "a vile man."[95]

In the Great Awakening section, if is said of George Whitefield, "Because he denounced the corrupt and unbiblical practices of the Anglican church, he was barred from most churches in England."[96]

During the Revolution, "Nearly all the religious leaders except the Anglicans opposed British domination. . ."[97] Nothing is mentioned about Anglican patriots like Washington, Henry and Madison, who supported independence. "Christians fought in apparently good conscience on both sides of the War for Independence. It must be noted, however, that the Anglican clergymen, who generally sided with Britain, were clearly outnumbered by the clergy of the more evangelical denominations, who were Patriot in sympathy."[98]

Students are never told that two thirds of the signers of the Declaration of Independence and the largest number of U.S. Presidents have been Episcopalians, though the contributions of other groups (Baptists, Methodists and Presbyterians in particular) are cited.

Students are reminded, though, that "without constitutional safeguards, the Church of England would destroy evangelical churches."[99]

Unfavorable accounts of the Church of England are numerous. We are informed in one text that, "As evangelical fervor died out in the established church and even in dissenting Protestant congregations, religious skepticism became more and more a threat to orthodoxy. By midcentury a desupernaturalized faith known as deism had made deep inroads into the English (Anglican) church, and religious toleration had become religious indifference among the laity."[100] "In the Anglican church, rationalism was taking hold and orthodoxy was deadening into traditionalism . . . Certain characteristics of Anglicanism were congenial to the slackening of evangelical faith. Anglican clergy generally assumed a regenerated congregation because of infant baptism and consequently did not preach the need of salvation as a personal instantaneous experience. The Anglican service manual (the *Book of Common Prayer*) contains the gospel but also a view of the ordinances of baptism and the Lord's Supper as sacraments, channeling grace to the participant. This view allows the ordinances to be regarded as contributing to salvation. In Anglican services the gospel, though grandly expressed, was easily overlaid by sacramentalism and ritual."[101] As a result, "Such religion had little effect upon upper-class morality and left the masses little better than barbarians."[102] In the nineteenth century "The evangelicals, like biblical fundamentalists today, were despised and when possible ignored by traditionalists and rationalists both within and without the Church of England."[103]

The Anglican priest and satirist Jonathan Swift is viewed critically. "His theology evidently did not grip him. His friendship with Pope, a Catholic, and with Bolingbroke, a freethinking deist and debauchee, reveals a dangerous separation between his religious beliefs and his intellectual life. It also shows a tolerance toward Romanism and rationalism within the

eighteenth-century Anglican church."[104]   Samuel Taylor
Coleridge's religion is dismissed haughtily. "Full satisfaction in
life and riddance of guilt are not within the power of transcendentalism to offer, and Coleridge, unlike Johnson, evidently
never found assurance of forgiveness through faith in
Christ."[105]

Those who regard the English *Book of Common Prayer*
as a masterpiece of the English language and a monumental
literary achievement will no doubt be baffled by its description
as "a quaint relic of an age of belief. To many of God's people
today it smacks of religious formalism in general and of
Catholicism in particular."[106] In another passage we read, "To
twentieth-century Fundamentalists King Edward's prayer book
would seem to have a Romish flavor . . ."[107] The description
of the successive prayer books[108] is grossly inaccurate and
reveals a limited acquaintance with Anglican liturgy on the part
of the author.

Once again, as with the entire Bob Jones University
series, this text raises the serious ethical question of having
individuals who are innately hostile to certain religious traditions
placed in the authorial position of describing someone else's
cherished religious convictions in a grossly distorted and
inaccurate manner. Students absorbing the erroneous information in this text cannot be expected to have any appreciation or
understanding for Anglican or Roman Catholic Christianity—
especially when they have been presented with a caricature rather
than an objective portrait. Anglicans, in particular, will find the
discussion of the Eucharist or the Holy Communion offensive
and incomplete. The author does admit that the Prayer Book
"has enriched our religious and cultural heritage,"[109] at the
same time distorting its theological base.

Several Anglican poets are discussed. Robert Herrick
"fashioned a neopagan world in which to play out his most
unchurchmanlike fantasies."[110] George Herbert, on the other
hand, is more pious and Protestant, though both Herrick and
Herbert were ordained Anglican clerics. Without citing any

factual evidence to support his claim, the author says this about Herbert, "Recent scholarship has shown Herbert to have been critical of the Catholic direction of the church and has placed his devotional poetry in the Protestant meditative tradition of Richard Baxter and his predecessors rather than in the Catholic tradition of Ignatius Loyola."[111]

After spending pages trying to prove that the Church of England was Protestant rather than Catholic but nonpapal, the author soon changes direction and charges that King Charles I "set out to Catholicize the Anglican service and found a willing servant in the haughty, tenacious William Laud, archbishop of Canterbury."[112] Archbishop Laud is said to have forced "a further Catholicized Book of Common Prayer"[113] on the people. (His brutal execution is omitted from the text.)

The Church of England also had other problems. "The Anglican church during this period felt the inroads of unbelief as well as of false belief."[114]

Because of its alleged Protestant influence, "Tudor literature offers more to God's people than British literature of any other period. . ."[115] This text waxes eloquent in its praise of John Milton, John Bunyan, George Herbert, and the King James Version of the Bible, whose translators, we are assured, believed "in the verbal inspiration of the original manuscripts."[116] The author cannot help criticizing modern Bible translators as he praises the translators of the King James Bible, ignoring the fact that King James I and most of the King James Version translators were themselves Anglicans. "In addition to splendid scholarship, the revisers possessed evangelical zeal and a feeling for language—two qualities rare among biblical translators today. Their evangelical zeal derived from the vitality of the Reformation tradition."[117]

John Donne's poetry receives praise, one suspects, only because Donne converted from Roman Catholicism to Anglicanism, yet Donne's complex poetry is still not quite Protestant enough. "The best of the sacred poems transcend the showmanship of his youth and the residual Catholic pietism of his age to express with great honesty and intensity the spiritual trials and victories of the Christian life."[118]

It is unlikely that students will perceive anything of spiritual or cultural value in the Anglican tradition after absorbing this material.

JEWS

Surprisingly, Jews and Judaism are almost invisible in these volumes. No mention is made of any Jewish contribution to U.S. history nor are any Jewish personalities in literature, sports or the arts mentioned. There is no reference to Justices Frankfurter, Brandeis or Cardozo. The only Jews mentioned are Karl Marx, who is called "an atheistic German Jew,"[119] and Sigmund Freud. It is noted that Jews were persecuted in Catholic countries but nothing is said about anti-Jewish discrimination in Protestant countries. Jewish supporters of Columbus are mentioned, as is the suggestion that Columbus may have been seeking a refuge for Jews.

One passage in a world history text, however, blames Jews for the crucifixion of Jesus. "The Jewish religious leaders, whose blindness and hypocrisy Jesus had denounced, sought to put Him to death. They brought Christ before the Roman governor Pontius Pilate, charging that Christ had disrupted the state. . . . Although Pilate found no fault in Jesus, he desired to maintain the peace. Giving in to the Jewish demands, he sentenced Jesus to death by crucifixion."[120] In addition, we are informed, "God used the destruction of Jerusalem to separate the early church from its Jewish environment and to scatter Christians throughout the Roman Empire."[121]

And one strange passage in a biology text says, "The Jews were pruned for the Gentiles' sake, but they were also pruned because of their disbelief."[122]

MUSLIMS, BUDDHISTS, AND HINDUS

Islam, Buddhism and Hinduism are treated with contempt in a major world history text. In a section on Islamic civilization, Muhammad's writings and contributions are labeled "so-called revelations," "claims" and "alleged" events.[123] The text summarizes Islam in this way. "But while Muhammad used many biblical terms in his teaching, he distorted biblical truth. Satan often uses this tactic to deceive people—he dresses error in the clothes of truth. Muhammad claimed to worship the same God as the Christians. But the god of the Koran is not the God of the Bible . . ."[124] Islamic paradise is ridiculed as a place in which "the 'faithful' will enjoy gardens of delight, rivers of wine, and the company of beautiful women."[125] Finally, "Islam seems to reflect those characteristics of false prophecy and teaching shown in II Peter 2:1-2."[126] The text does admit that Islamic culture made some contributions to civilization, particularly in medicine and mathematics. But the student clearly knows that the Islamic religion is false. This is rein-forced by this instruction to students: "List the Five Pillars of Islam and next to each write what the Bible teaches about it. (For example, the first is wrong because of Exodus 20:3 and John 3:18.)"[127]

When Indian civilization is introduced, the religious traditions of Hinduism and Buddhism are labeled "pagan."[128] "Both Hindus and Buddhists believe that man can achieve eternal peace if his good works outweigh his bad. The followers of these pagan religions never know, however, if they have done more good works than bad. Moreover, they fail to realize that even a large number of good works cannot erase the fact of sin. The only remedy for man's sin is God's saving grace."[129]

THE CHINESE RELIGIONS

Though the philosophy of Confucius is praised grudgingly for containing "morally sound advice,"[130] his religion cannot escape criticism. "The major defect in Confucius's teaching was his neglect of the most important relationship of all—man and God. Only as we fulfill our duties and responsibilities to God are we able to properly fulfill those to our fellow men."[131] The other indigenous Chinese religion, Taoism, is said to have become "the basis of mystical, magical, and superstitious elements in Chinese society."[132]   Asian religions are deemed worthless because "The Asians relied upon human tradition in determining what is true and good. Paul warns of this danger in Colossians 2:8."[133]   And, "The cultures of India, China, and Japan are among the oldest and most enduring in the world today. They are also among the most heathen. This is not to say they are nonreligious, for Hinduism, Buddhism, Confucianism, Taoism, and Shintoism played an important role in shaping the lives of the people in the Orient. But in these lands the vast majority of people live apart from the knowledge of God and His truth. Instead of worshipping the true living God, they follow after polytheism, idols, superstition, vain philosophies, myths, and fables. Their man-centered religions offer no hope beyond this life. Only in Christ can man look to the future with confidence and expectation."[134]

These texts are nothing if not up to date in their condemnations of false doctrines. A 1991 biology text claims that the New Age Movement "has ensnared many unsaved people and led astray many Christians."[135]   Transcendental Meditation, it is said, does not bring "real lasting strength, peace and joy but only Satan's counterfeit."[136]

In the narrow little world of fundamentalist schools, virtually the entire spectrum of faith is seen as an enemy, not as fellow searchers after truth or collaborators toward a better world. They are seen as heretics doomed to eternal punishment.

NOTES

1. Michael R. Lowman, *United States History in Christian Perspective* (Pensacola, FL: Pensacola Christian College, 1983), p. 221.

2. *Ibid.*, p. 221.

3. Raymond A. St. John, *American Literature for Christian Schools, Book 2, (Realism, Naturalism, and Modern American Literature)*, Teacher's Edition (Greenville, SC: Bob Jones University Press, 1991), p. 541.

4. Rachel C. Larson with Pamela Creason, *The American Republic for Christian Schools*, (Greenville, SC: Bob Jones University Press, 1988), p. 62.

5. *Ibid.*, p. 446.

6. *Ibid.*, p. 446.

7. Raymond A. St. John, *American Literature for Christian Schools, Book 1, (Early American Literature and American Romanticism)*, Teacher's Edition (Greenville, SC: Bob Jones University Press, 1991), p. 2.

8. Lowman, p. 224.

9. *Ibid.*, p. 226.

10. *Ibid.*, p. 490.

11. *Ibid.*, p. 503.

12. *Ibid.*, p. 502.

13. *Ibid.*, p. 503.

14. St. John, p. 341.

15. *Ibid.*, p. 341.

16. *Ibid.*, p. 342.

17. *Ibid.*, p. 342.

18. *Ibid.*, p. 541.

19. *Ibid.*, p. 541.

20. *Ibid.*, p. 541.

21. *Ibid.*, p. 541.

22. *Ibid.*, p. 542.

23. Larson and Creason, p. 447.

24. *Ibid.*, p. 425.

25. *Ibid.*, p. 987-99T.

26. *Ibid.*, p. 446.

27. *Ibid.*, p. 62.

28. *Ibid.*, p. 203.

29. *Ibid.*, p. 203.

30. *Ibid.*, p. 378.

31. *Ibid.*, p. 397.

32. *Ibid.*, p. 398.

33. *Ibid.*, p. 439.

34. *Ibid.*, p. 439.

35. St. John, *American Literature for Christian Schools, Book 1*, p. 144.

36. *Ibid.*, p. 143.

37. Lowman, p. 221.

38. Larson and Creason, p. 276.

39. *Ibid.*, p. 62.

40. *Ibid.*, p. 276.

41. *Ibid.*, p. 62.

42. *Ibid.*, p. 277.

43. *Ibid.*, p. 61T.

44. *Ibid.*, p. 60T.

45. *Ibid.*, p. 276.

46. *Ibid.*, p. 275.

47. Raymond A. St. John, *American Literature for Christian Schools, Book 2*, Teachers Edition (Greenville, SC, Bob Jones University Press, 1991), p. 438.

48. *Ibid.*, p. 538.

49. *Ibid.*, p. 539.

50. *Ibid.*, p. 539.

51. David A. Fisher, *World History for Christian Schools*, (Greenville, SC: Bob Jones University Press, 1984), p. 264.

52. *Ibid.*, p. 484.

53. Glen Chambers and Gene Fisher, *United States History for Christian Schools*, (Greenville, SC: Bob Jones University Press, 1982), pp. 443-444.

54. William S. Pinkston, Jr., *Biology for Christian Schools*, (Greenville, SC: Bob Jones University Press, 1991), p. 651.

55. Jan Anderson and Laurel Hicks, *The Literature of the American People, Vol. 4*, A Beka Book (Pensacola, FL: Pensacola Christian College Press, 1983), p. 252.

56. Michael R. Lowman, *United States History in Christian Perspective*, A Beka Book (Pensacola, FL: Pensacola Christian College, 1983), p. 506.

57. *Ibid.*, p. 595-96.

58. *Ibid.*, p. 599.

59. Chambers and Fisher, p. 240.

60. *Ibid.*, p. 240.

61. *Ibid.*, p. 240.

62. Larson and Creason, p. 63T.

63. *Ibid.*, p. 282.

64. Chambers and Fisher, pp. 48-49.

65. *Ibid.*, p. 72.

66. *Ibid.*, p. 74.

67. David A. Fisher, *World History for Christian Schools* (Greenville, SC: Bob Jones University Press, 1984), p. 130.

68. *Ibid.*, p. 131.

69. *Ibid.*, p. 135.

70. *Ibid.*, p. 136.

71. *Ibid.*, p. 137.

72. Ronald A. Horton, *British Literature for Christian Schools: The Modern Tradition, 1688 to the Present* (Greenville, SC: Bob Jones University Press, 1982), p. 368.

73. Jan Anderson and Laurel Hicks, *The Literature of England, Classics for Christians, Vol. 6*, (Pensacola, FL: Pensacola Christian College, 1983), pp. 3-4.

74. *Ibid.*, p. 4.

75. *Ibid.*, p. 58.

76. *Ibid.*, p. 58.

77. *Ibid.*, p. 58.

78. *Ibid.*, p. 59.

79. *Ibid.*, p. 100.

80. *Ibid.*, p. 100.

81. *Ibid.*, p. 100.

82. *Ibid.*, p. 101.
83. *Ibid.*, p. 375.
84. *Ibid.*, p. 244.
85. *Ibid.*, p. 244.
86. *Ibid.*, p. 245.
87. Glen Chambers and Gene Fisher, *United States History for Christian Schools* (Greenville, SC: Bob Jones University Press, 1982), p. 38.
88. *Ibid.*, p. 38.
89. *Ibid.*, p. 50.
90. *Ibid.*, p. 69.
91. *Ibid.*, p. 69.
92. *Ibid.*, p. 69.
93. *Ibid.*, p. 69.
94. *Ibid.*, p. 74.
95. *Ibid.*, p. 81.
96. *Ibid.*, p. 85.
97. *Ibid.*, p. 117.
98. *Ibid.*, p. 124.
99. *Ibid.*, p. 117.
100. Horton, p. 4.
101. *Ibid.*, p. 9.
102. *Ibid.*, p. 10.
103. *Ibid.*, p. 265.
104. *Ibid.*, p. 46.
105. *Ibid., p. 201.*
106. Ronald A. Horton, *British Literature for Christian Schools: The Early Tradition, 700-1688* (Greenville, SC: Bob Jones University Press, 1980), p. 186.
107. *Ibid.*, p. 149.
108. *Ibid.*, pp. 186-190.
109. *Ibid.*, p. 189.
110. *Ibid.*, p. 325.
111. *Ibid.*, p. 328.
112. *Ibid.*, p. 290.
113. *Ibid.*, p. 292.

114. *Ibid.*, p. 297.

115. *Ibid.*, p. 300.

116. *Ibid.*, p. 304.

117. *Ibid.*, p. 305.

118. *Ibid.*, p. 316.

119. Chambers and Fisher, p. 350.

120. Fisher, pp. 109-110.

121. *Ibid.*, p. 112.

122. William S. Pinkston, Jr., *Biology for Christian Schools, Book 1*, Teacher's Edition (Greenville, SC: Bob Jones University Press, 1991), p. 333.

123. Fisher, pp. 139-140.

124. *Ibid.*, p. 141.

125. *Ibid.*, p. 141.

126. *Ibid.*, p. 142.

127. *Ibid.*, p. 147.

128. *Ibid.*, p. 151.

129. *Ibid.*, p. 153.

130. *Ibid.*, p. 159.

131. *Ibid.*, p. 158.

132. *Ibid.*, p. 160.

133. *Ibid.*, p. 167.

134. *Ibid.*, p. 168.

135. Williams S. Pinkston, Jr., *Biology for Christian Schools, Book 2*, Teacher's Edition, (Greenville, SC: Bob Jones University Press, 1991), p. 611.

136. *Ibid.*, p. 615.

2

NO POPERY

The Roman Catholic Church is the *bête noire* of fundamentalist textbook writers. In history, literature, geography, and science, Catholic-bashing is an acceptable and seemingly indispensable method of instruction.

In world history the students are only informed about the features of Catholic faith, culture, and practice which are deemed objectionable or heretical by fundamentalists. There is no attempt made to understand the historical development of Christianity, or the mutations which it underwent as it emerged from Palestine to become the dominant force and culture of European civilization.

The student learns nothing about the writings of early church fathers, the rise of the Papacy, the conflicts between church and state, the development of religious calendars and holy days, basilica architecture, theological controversies, the development of a cult of honor accorded to martyrs and confessors, liturgy, or church government. What is taught is essentially caricature.

Let us begin with a major world history text utilized by these schools. The early Christian church is seen in the light of later historical polemicism. A heavy emphasis is placed on the adoption of "pagan ideas and practices" into the church without explaining at least the rationale of church authorities for incorporating elements of other traditions and giving them new interpretations. Monasticism, for example, is seen as being "not of Christian origin nor biblically based but from the eastern pagan religions."[1]

The classic fundamentalist view of church history is adopted. "Because of the close ties between church and state, the worldliness of many Christians, the adoption of pagan ideas, and religious hierarchy, the church gradually departed from the truth of the Christian faith. The seeds of error that took root during the fourth and fifth centuries blossomed during the Middle Ages into the Roman Catholic church—a perversion of biblical Christianity."[2] A sidebar on Augustine of Hippo is included, though readers would never know that he was a canonized saint of the Catholic church, a disciple of St. Ambrose of Milan, a foe of the dissenting Christian movement called Donatism and of African descent.

When we come to the history of medieval Christendom, we reach the forbidden realm, the epoch which fundamentalist Protestants find most fearsome and evil, and the historical era which they most delight in ridiculing.

The author of this world history text is obviously uncomfortable in dealing with historical facts which disturb him. He is not sure just when the concept of catholicity began. "It is difficult to tell precisely when the 'universal church' as perceived by Europeans took on the official title of the Roman Catholic church. One thing is certain, however: the *true* universal church and the Roman Catholic church are not synonymous."[3] Oddly, he does not even mention the numerous "heresies" that vied for hegemony with the "orthodox" or catholic traditions during the age of the seven ecumenical councils, when church doctrine was debated and defined.

Throughout this entire section Roman Catholic traditions and practices are incorrectly defined or distorted. There is no attempt at understanding why Roman Catholics (and the Eastern

Orthodox) believed as they did or interpreted the Scriptures as they did. The belief in the papacy is said to rest "upon a number of false assumptions"[4] because "There is no historical evidence that Peter ever served as the bishop of the church at Rome."[5] This confusion is compounded later when Gregory I is said to be "commonly recognized as the first true pope."[6]

There are sweeping generalizations about medieval Christian life. "Although there was much church activity, there was little true faith. The church had compromised with the world. Because few people other than the clergy could read and examine the Bible for themselves, the majority of the people placed their trust in the visible church instead of in Christ; they looked to an institution for guidance instead of to the Word of God. Christians began to tolerate spiritual error; without the Bible, they knew no better. Gradually their faith became separated from the truth, and they believed in a distortion of biblical Christianity. This period is perhaps best characterized as an age of spiritual ignorance and darkness."[7] Pope Gregory was "blinded by superstition and ignorance."[8] In addition, "the Roman Catholic church in its long history has given increasing importance to the traditions of man at the expense of God's truth. During the Middle Ages, the church was more interested in preserving outward unity among its members than in fostering the inner peace that comes by faith in Jesus Christ. Gradually people began to look to this institutional church for salvation, rather than to the Saviour, Jesus Christ."[9]

The church is depicted as a wholly corrupt institution. "The Roman church, with the pope as its head, assumed the role of mediator between God and man, between this world and the world to come. It claimed to be the guardian of truth and the final authority in interpreting the Scriptures. The Roman church believed in the inspiration and authority of the Bible as God's Word, but it contended that the traditions of the church had equal authority. As a result, the doctrine and practice of the Roman church was a dangerous mixture of truth and error."[10]

The veneration of saints, which many historians trace to the second or third century emphasis on martyrs, confessors, and intercessory prayer, is called "one of the greatest errors promoted by the Roman church during the Middle Ages."[11] Devotion to the Virgin Mary is called "worship,"[12] though Roman Catholic and Orthodox theologians have long stressed the distinctions between *latria* (adoration of God), and veneration (*dulia*) of the saints and *hyperdulia* for the Virgin Mary.

To medieval man Mary "became more important than Christ Himself."[13]

The description of the seven sacraments[14] is incomplete, unsatisfactory and distorted. There is no attempt at fairness or understanding. Students are never informed that many Christian groups believe the seven sacraments can be legitimately traced to specific New Testament passages. Readers of this text can only assume that sacraments were invented by later church rulers to deceive and enslave the ignorant, as in this passage: "Because of the Roman sacramental system, salvation became a product of works, not a matter of faith. The church taught that only by participating in the sacraments could one have any hope of heaven and only through the sacraments could God be properly worshiped. The words of Jesus Christ show the error of this system. . ."[15]

The text gleefully regales readers with a discussion of the abuses of relics in the Middle Ages. "It was such a superstition that blinded minds of the people in the Middle Ages to the truth of God's Word."[16]

The anti-Catholic animus is occasionally mitigated by little oddities. St. Patrick "took the gospel to Ireland"[17] but St. Jerome's Vulgate translation of the Bible is "somewhat inaccurate."[18] A surprising admission is made in reference to the book repeatedly called infallible and inerrant by the author. "By the fourth century there had been so many mistakes in translating and copying the Scriptures that many Latin manuscripts were no longer reliable."[19] Still, the hand of God theory appears time and again.   "God used the Carolingian scholars to preserve copies of the Bible."[20]

In the section covering the ninth through the thirteenth centuries, much material is devoted to "corrupt popes and worldly clergy,"[21] portraits of the church "sunk deep in moral corruption,"[22] and depictions of the "inept and immoral men" who "openly committed great wickedness"[23] in the papacy. Simony,[24] excommunications, interdicts, and inquisitions[25] are characteristic of the papacy.

In a discussion on church-state conflicts in the Middle Ages, the author claims that "Satan encourages this conflict even today as he attempts to harm God's people and frustrate God's purposes."[26]

Reform movements within the church are dismissed. "Sadly, many medieval reformers devoted more effort to rebuilding the church's prestige than to restoring its purity. . . . Though churchmen made outward changes, they failed to recognize the need for inward cleansing and forgiveness through Jesus Christ. They failed to see that genuine reform is possible only for regenerate hearts."[27]

About the Crusades we read: "The popes proclaimed that participation in the Crusades was a substitute for penance. Hardened sinners were told they could earn forgiveness of sins by joining one of these campaigns. Furthermore, the Roman church assured the Crusaders that anyone who died while on a Crusade would be granted eternal life. Of course this was a false assurance, given by church leaders who manipulated the credulous people. Notice the similarity of this false teaching of the Roman church to that of the Islamic religion."[28]

At times the book seems to praise the Catholic Church's contributions to art, music, and architecture. Medieval hymnody is praised and stained-glass windows were called a kind of "visual Bible."[29] But the writer cannot avoid making theological interpretations and suppositions. In a discussion about symbolism in medieval art, we read, "In this painting entitled *The Coronation of the Virgin*, the Italian artist Antonia da Imola portrays the Roman Catholic myth of the crowning of the Virgin Mary as Queen of Heaven. A number of Bible characters and medieval 'saints' are gathered around Christ and Mary watching this 'event.' Like many other works of art from the Middle Ages, this painting reflects a mixture of biblical truth and Romanist error."[30]

The scholastic philosophers "neglected the Bible as the source of faith and the guide for reason."[31] Therefore, "In their attempts to explain their faith the scholastics revealed many contradictions in the church's teaching. . . . In this way God used the scholastics to prepare for the coming of the Reformation."[32]

The Chambers and Fisher volume for American history courses, proclaiming that "Catholicism Enslaves Man," says: "During the first three centuries after Christ's ascension, believers withstood severe persecution by the Roman Empire and took the message of the cross to most of Europe. But in A.D. 313 persecution ceased when the Roman emperor Constantine, claiming to have seen a vision of a cross in the sky, decreed Christianity a legal religion. Unopposed by the secular government, Christianity waned. Its spiritual muscles became flabby; the weakened body of Christ faced infection and corruption. Roman emperor—sinful men—supplanted the sinless Son of God as organized Christianity's head. From this corrupted system emerged the Roman Catholic church. . ."[33]

The text continues, "In spite of genuine believers within its ranks, the Roman church hastened the coming of ignorance by keeping much religious knowledge behind monastery doors, away from the 'laity.' In 1229 the church decreed that only the clergy could understand the Bible; thus the clergy alone were permitted to possess it. Laymen were limited to scant portions of Scripture in Latin, a language that they could not have understood even had they been able to read. Those who exalted the Bible above church teachings were persecuted, and their Bibles were destroyed. . . . During the fifteenth and sixteenth centuries, the Roman church destroyed more Bibles than the pagan emperors had destroyed during the first five centuries of church history. Thus the Roman Catholic system ensured the people's intellectual and spiritual ignorance by depriving them of God's infallible Word and placing in their hands instead the traditions of fallible men."[34]

It is then asserted that God used the Renaissance and the printing press to weaken Catholicism.

"The first of two movements God used to destroy the monopoly of Catholicism was the Renaissance, or 'rebirth,' which began in the fourteenth century and developed into a reaction to Rome's educational and cultural tyranny. Although the Renaissance over-emphasized the worth of human nature, it broke the church's educational monopoly and advanced man's knowledge.[35] . . . Despite its overly exalted view of man, the Renaissance helped to restore the Scriptures to the common people."[36]

Soon thereafter, "God used several men, whom we call pre-Reformers, . . . to proclaim his Word and to oppose the Church's errors."[37]

Martin Luther is seen as a saintly hero who, "while visiting the 'Holy City' of Rome, was thoroughly disappointed by the Roman clergy's materialistic and worldly attitudes. From then on he realized that much of the conduct and teaching of the Roman church was blasphemous and that a victorious Christian life—like salvation—stemmed from faith.

"As Luther's faith matured, he became more aware of Rome's errors, especially the selling of indulgences."[38] Afterwards, "he refused to acknowledge that the pope's decrees were equal to the Word of God. His firm stand brought him excommunication, but God spared his life. He translated the entire Bible into German, promoted education for all youth, and emphasized salvation by grace alone. . . . God used Luther to break Rome's hold by establishing biblical authority over papal authority and replacing Rome's pagan system of works with the biblical teaching of Christ's atoning work on the cross."[39]

Ulrich Zwingli, a Swiss reformer, is praised because "His presentation of the gospel caused many to look beyond Catholic ritual to Christ and to be converted. . . . His clear preaching virtually eliminated Roman Catholicism in Zurich."[40] The text fails to mention that it was the civil government which ruthlessly eliminated Catholicism in Zurich and Geneva, as well as putting Unitarian leader Michael Servetus to death.

John Calvin is another hero. "Perhaps no other person had as much influence upon colonial America as did Reformer John Calvin. He emphasized God's sovereignty, man's depravity, salvation by grace, church discipline, and individual accountability to God. He also taught the dignity of hard work and the profit motive. . . .Calvin was brilliant, modest, aloof, and unsaved. When first presented with the gospel, he rejected it; but the Holy Spirit continued to work in his heart, and he was saved when about twenty-two.[41] . . . Unlike Luther, who had intended only to reform the Roman church, Calvin insisted that believers should separate from it."[42]

John Knox preached in Scotland and won "many to Christ and of course away from the Catholic church."[43] Therefore, "Bible-honoring Presbyterian churches continued to grow in Scotland long after Knox's death."[44]

The significance of this background for Americans is described in this way.

"Our nation's heritage is deeply rooted in the Protestant Reformation. The early settlers were predominantly Protestants who opposed both the Roman church and all other churches that placed man's authority above that of Scripture. Many also wanted to reach the inhabitants of the New World with the gospel. Early colonists established churches and governments that were relatively free from tyranny."[45]

Even paintings in the text are used to attack the Catholic artistic imagination. A painting of *The Nativity* by Ghirlandaio is described thusly, "The Catholic church used art to reinforce many of the doctrines that the Reformers found objectionable.

The halo, for example, was used to encourage veneration of the saints."[46]

The treatment of the Reformation in all of these books is deficient. No attention is given to the sociological, economic, cultural, geographic or political factors which predisposed certain nations toward acceptance of Reformation theology and social organization. Students are told that God intervened directly in history to bring about this event, and no further discussion is needed. This is a grossly unacceptable way to teach students the meaning and matter of history.

There is also surprisingly little discussion of such politically influential Protestant principles as private judgment in the interpretation of the Scriptures. These texts continually tell students what certain Biblical passages mean, and no dissent is encouraged.

Stereotypes continue in a discussion of Christopher Columbus. While professing not to know Columbus's motives, the text assures us: "Columbus's *Book of the Prophecies* makes it clear that he was a devout student of the Bible. In this book, as one of his reasons for his explorations, he urges the quick spread of the gospel because of the shortness of time. Yet many of his statements employ Roman terminology; for example, he speaks of Isaiah's prophecy as intended 'to call all people to our holy catholic faith.' (By Columbus's time, the word *catholic* referred almost exclusively to the Roman church.) He may have been less than sincere, however; the Roman church's influence during Columbus's time forced most Spaniards to appear to be devout Roman Catholics, regardless of their true beliefs. Whether he was a true Christian or only a devout Catholic, though, Columbus believed that his decision to sail west resulted from God's leading."[47]

This analysis of Columbus raises interesting questions. If Columbus was such a serious student of the Bible, how did he obtain a copy in the vernacular language when the authors of this text claim time and again that Catholics were forbidden to read the Scriptures on their own? How did Columbus study the Bible if Catholic authorities in Spain prohibited the publication, sale and distribution of the Scriptures, as they claim? And how did Columbus come to appreciate the Gospel, and support its expansion, if Catholicism was so horrible and depraved a religion?

Since the authors cannot admit that any Catholic could be decent, sincere, humane, or truly Christian, they try to suggest that Columbus was not really a Catholic. He only pretended to be one to gain royal approval. The authors cannot admit to themselves nor will they allow students to infer that Columbus may have been a sincere Christian and a Catholic—something these authors believe is impossible.

Students are continually reminded that the early Spanish and French Catholics were a potential threat to the Protestant English colonies. "Pagan Catholicism replaced the Aztec's pagan practices . . . and the Aztecs continued to live in fear and spiritual darkness."[48] Also, "While Spain was conquering much of the Western Hemisphere, France was preoccupied with exterminating the French Protestants, the Huguenots."[49]

Sir Walter Raleigh "was distressed that the Spanish Catholics were winning the American Indians to their 'noxious' religion. . ."[50]

Maryland's Catholic governors are given only grudging credit for passing the first religious freedom guarantee in the colonies. "In order to give liberty to the Catholics and still entice Protestant settlers, the colony's leaders established religious toleration through the Toleration Act of 1649, which provided that no one professing a belief in Christ should be troubled in the free exercise of his religion. Since the Catholic leaders were soon outnumbered by Protestant settlers, the act was indeed wise; by 1776 only one percent were Catholics."[51] Actually, Maryland was 15% Catholic in 1776. The text says further, "The act quieted controversy for a time and encouraged the continued increase in Protestant settlement."[52]

The text never mentions that Maryland Catholics were ruthlessly persecuted after 1692, were forbidden to worship openly, to educate their children, were disarmed and double taxed and were forbidden to vote or hold public office. Most of these restrictions applied to the other 13 colonies, but students reading the Bob Jones University text will never know that, either.

Maryland is dismissed as merely a propaganda center for Catholics. "Protestants outnumbered Catholics from the beginning, although Catholics controlled Maryland's government. Jesuit missionaries were then imported and won many of the settlers and neighboring Indians to Catholicism."[53] Even after the Protestant Establishment, "Maryland remained a Roman Catholic base from which Catholic missionaries would work in the future."[54] This presentation of Maryland falls far short of accuracy.

While the expulsion of five thousand Acadians from Nova Scotia by the British in the 1750s is mentioned, the factor of religious prejudice is omitted. [55]

The passage of the Quebec Act by Parliament in 1774 is seen as "establishing the Roman Catholic Church in Quebec" and "encircling the Protestant colonies with Catholicism."[56]

The only passage in the entire 648-page book which is even slightly fair to Catholics is the portrait of Governor Alfred E. Smith's presidential bid in 1928. "Republicans also attacked Smith's Roman Catholic background. Many of the attacks were prompted by a genuine concern over possible threats to Protestantism; others resulted from sheer bigotry. Many of the charges were shoddy, unreasonable accusations that could not have come from a genuine concern to preserve religious liberty."[57]

Another example of religious bias is the portrait of the French and Indian War as a "war for religious freedom."[58] "The French and Indian wars were more than merely a struggle for a geographic empire; they were in part an effort to preserve a biblical Protestantism in America. A French victory would result in a Catholic North America; with a British victory the land would remain Protestant."[59]

An obscure, and possibly apocryphal, event, is then described in a calculated effort to create fear of Catholics. It purportedly comes from "the diary of John Williams, a Puritan preacher from Deerfield, Mass." "Once the group arrived in Canada, they were turned over to Jesuit priests, who were even more cruel than the Indians. In the spirit of the Inquisition, they tried almost every method imaginable to force the captives to become Catholics. Of course the most obvious means, like torture and intimidation, were used. Other methods, however, were more devious. Williams was promised that his three children would be released if he would convert. Others were told that their friends had become Catholics just before dying under Jesuit torture. Despite these efforts, few actually converted.

"Despite the physical and mental torture, and despite the fact that he was not allowed to see a copy of the Scriptures, Williams remained faithful."[60]

This viewpoint reappears later in the chapter. "Perhaps the most significant result of the war was that it determined that America would be a Protestant nation that would offer both religious and civil liberty to its people. Bible-preaching Protestant churches, many of which resulted from the Great Awakening, produced people with the moral character necessary to maintain these liberties. If France had won, it seems fairly certain that America would have become a Catholic nation and would, of necessity, have been forced to live under the combined absolutism of church and state. Early Americans would have been taught a 'gospel' of works rather than the gospel of grace through faith in the Lord Jesus Christ."[61]

An absurd assertion is the claim that one factor in the Civil War was the South's desire to retain its Protestant identity. There was "a rise in Unitarianism, Catholicism, and Transcendentalism. The Southern states, which are even today called the 'Bible Belt,' saw themselves threatened by those holding these unbiblical beliefs, who were most numerous in the Northeast."[62]

This charge lacks any historical foundation. Both North and South were heavily Protestant. Catholics served in both armies, and as generals in both armies. The most heavily Catholic state in those days was Louisiana, a Confederate state. Furthermore, marauding Union troops engaged in several instances of Catholic church burnings in their invasion of the South. Troops from Know-Nothing dominated regions of New England were particularly prone to this activity, which gave Southern propagandists in Europe, especially Ireland, a strong argument against the Union. Finally, the Cabinet of Jefferson Davis was far more religiously pluralistic than that of Abraham Lincoln. A Catholic (Stephen Mallory) and a Jew (Judah P. Benjamin) served in the highest echelons of the Confederate government, while Lincoln's Cabinet was entirely Protestant. It is also of some interest that a leading Southern secessionist before the War was a Unitarian, Vice-President John C. Calhoun.

Immigrants to the United States are accorded only minimal treatment, mostly favorable when they were from Protestant lands in Northern Europe, but unfavorable when they hailed from other countries.

The immigrants to New York were "hardworking and thrifty Protestant refugees from the Spanish (southern) Netherlands."[63] The Huguenots are praised. "Another group that suffered for its biblical beliefs and contributed to the establishment of our American liberties was the French Huguenots. Persecuted by Catholic rulers, many thousands of Protestant Huguenots left France; and many of those later came to America. France's loss became America's gain; many of the Huguenots had been the most intelligent and skilled people in France. In essence, the Catholics selected the cultural cream of France and donated it to America."[64] The Germans are admired. "Some came from Germany after Louis XIV deliberately destroyed food supplies in a predominantly Protestant area of Germany in an attempt to gain control of the region. The

French king's purpose was to force the inhabitants into Catholicism; he forced them into America instead."[65]

While immigrants are occasionally praised, "immigration aggravated labor unrest"[66] and "immigrants were widely resented, for a number of reasons."[67]   The main reason was that "many immigrants, especially those from southeastern Europe, were Roman Catholic, a fact that aroused fear and resentment among Protestants and others who feared the potential political power of the Roman church."[68]

The Know-Nothing party is barely mentioned as "anti-slavery, anti-Catholic and anti-immigrant,"[69] but no attention is given to the anti-Catholic terrorism mounted by Nativists and Know-Nothings during the 1840s and 1850s, which led to church burnings and violence in Philadelphia and other cities. Apparently, students reading this text are not supposed to know that Protestant nativists ever persecuted Catholics at any time in U.S. history.

Sympathy is also expressed for immigration restriction legislation.   The Emergency Quota Act of 1921 "failed to accomplish its purpose of limiting immigration from southeastern Europe, where Catholic and Bolshevist influences were particularly great."[70]   Therefore, the 1924 Immigration Act was a vital necessity.

Another U.S. history text takes a similar posture. Criticism of Roman Catholics marks the background material to colonial American life.   Catholicism in France is said to be "marked by superstition, cold formalism and lack of application to daily life."[71]

About Columbus's religion we are told: "Christopher Columbus was a devout Roman Catholic. He was very pious in his works of religion. It is said that he went through the daily official prayers and chants of the Roman church more than the average priest did, and yet his life was not marked by the honesty and moral uprightness we expect of a true Christian hero."[72]

Elsewhere, the apocrypha is defined as "a collection of books the Roman church added to the Bible."[73]   The apocrypha, a collection of books found in Roman Catholic and Eastern Orthodox Bibles and included in the first edition of the King James Version, is neither defined nor discussed in the text.

Catholicism is described as "a distorted Christianity that had largely departed from the teachings of the Bible."[74]   The text continues: "By A.D. 400, church and state had been united, and the result was that a few religious leaders were placed between God and the rest of mankind. The Bible was kept from the people; they were only told what church leaders in Rome wanted them to believe about the Scriptures. People were told that in order to go to heaven they must obey all the dictates of the Church of Rome."[75]

All of the relevant literature texts ridicule Catholic contributions to literature and extol the Protestant contributions.

Here are examples from an early British literature text. This text on early British literature includes numerous religious biases and defamatory statements aimed at Catholic Christianity. The selections from medieval and Elizabethan literature reflect these prejudices.

Of the 400 pages in the text barely 50 reflect the pre-Reformation period. Both Roman and Celtic Christianity (called Irish Catholicism) are labeled "spiritually bankrupt."[76] "Primitive Christianity came to England in the first century. . . . Unfortunately, the Celtic church during the Roman occupation followed the rest of Christendom into Catholic ritualism and superstition."[77]   Christian England is described as "a curious blend of pagan and Christian elements—not unusual, however, where Catholicism has assimilated a native culture."[78]   A patronizing tone is introduced in this sentence. "Within apostate Romanism were undoubtedly genuine believers who sought to please God according to the light that was granted them."[79]

A very brief and unrepresentative selection from Bede's *Ecclesiastical History* is preceded by a description of the Mass as "unbiblical and idolatrous" and as "a supposedly miraculous reenactment of the crucifixion."[80]   The students are also told that "the ministry of any human priest is unnecessary and fraudulent."[81]

Chaucer's contribution to literature is preceded by an attack on monasticism, which is portrayed in this way: "This mystic-ascetic flight from the world has no justification in Scripture but derives from pagan influences on apostate Christianity. . . . the Bible nowhere recommends a life of physical self-denial as a means of spiritual advancement."[82]   One wonders why Jesus spent 40 days fasting in the wilderness before beginning his public ministry. The passage ends, "Ascetic self-denial is usually the result not of spiritual humility but of carnal pride."[83]   Monks are among the book's favorite villains, as in this passage; "The friars, as a group, were the most fanatical enemies of the spread of evangelical Christianity in Catholic-dominated lands, opposing the circulation of the Scriptures in the vernacular and energetically furthering the papal inquisition."[84] The Reformation is presented as coming directly from God. "It was only a matter of time—God's time—until true religion, supported by secular power and popular enthusiasm, would break the hold of Catholicism in northern Europe."[85]

Geoffrey Chaucer's "The Nun's Priest's Tale" is included, since it satirizes aspects of religious life in the Middle Ages. This gives the text's author ample opportunity to continue his opprobrium.

Ignorance of the religious culture of England is revealed in several places. The term "Martinmas"[86] is defined as the "feast of St. Martin which commemorates the martyrdom of Pope Martin I in 655." In actual fact Martinmas celebrates the feast of St. Martin of Tours, a fourth century soldier in Gaul whose munificent acts of charity toward the poor and helpless made him a figure of great devotion in the Middle Ages. Francis X. Weiser described Martinmas as "the Thanksgiving Day of the Middle Ages, a holiday in Germany, France, Holland, England and Central Europe."[87]   St. Martin of Tours, says Charles Alexander, "has always been a popular saint in

England, where over a hundred and fifty churches are dedicated to him, including an old church at Canterbury dating from the Roman Christian days."[88]

The medieval morality and miracle plays and religious allegories are given an odd twist since the author is so uncomfortable with Catholic imagery. He constructs a false contrast between *Everyman* and Chaucer's Canterbury Tales: "The concept of Everyman as a pilgrim from life recalls Chaucer's representation of men as pilgrims through life. Whereas the destination of the Canterbury pilgrims is an earthly religious shrine, that of Everyman, as of Bunyan's Christian, is the very abode of God."[89]

The text's description of the Renaissance and Reformation periods is slanted. The students are given no opportunity to weigh contrasting opinions or to look prudently at historical events without being told what and how to think. The defeat of the Spanish Armada is called "a victory miraculously fashioned by the hand of God . . ."[90] The Reformation made England "not only a haven for persecuted Protestants but also a divine instrument for propagating religious truth in Catholic Europe and throughout the world."[91]

This religious viewpoint shapes the interpretation of English literature advanced in this book. "The literature of the later Tudor period," we are informed, "is permeated with biblical allusions and infused with Christian idealism" because "it had felt the impact of the Protestant Reformation."[92]

The treatment of Sir Thomas More and his classic *Utopia* reveals a mean-spirited religious vindictiveness. More is condemned for "his unrelenting opposition to spiritual truth and his religious bigotry,"[93] which in a textbook like this is equivalent to the pot calling the kettle black. "More's argumentative tactics show Catholic apologetics at their worst,"[94] we are informed. Even More's martyrdom is treated with disdain. "We can admire the courage with which More faced his death but still recall that Protestants had endured as much by his instigation."[95] His career is dismissed in these words: "Chiefly, his career illustrates the fact that worldly wisdom is no advantage—and, if grounded in pride, is a disadvantage—in the perception of spiritual truth."[96]

The Protestant controversialist and Bible-translator William Tyndale, on the other hand, is seen as one of England's greatest writers, renowned for his "plain, energetic language," "humble, idiomatic English" and "his ability to communicate to the common man."[97] In summary, "Tyndale's accomplishment as translator, expositor, and defender of the Word of truth shows the usefulness to God of the same intellectual gifts and scholarly training that turned More, in pride, against the gospel and aided his attempts to root out Protestantism in England."[98]

A similar volume from another publisher can be cited. While introducing Bede and Caedmon, the authors remind us that "a distorted form of Christianity prevailed" in those days.[99] Geoffrey Chaucer's era was a time of "graft and corruption" in the church.[100] Students read Chaucer's "The Pardoner's Tale" and "The Nun's Priest's Tale," which are the most critical of church life in fourteenth century England. The great play *Everyman* is labeled "unScriptural" because it advocates good works.[101]

"People were ignorant of what was going on" when they attended Mass, we are assured.[102]

The Reformation is portrayed as a wonderful era when truth was rediscovered. Students are told that "Henry VIII was used of God to further the Protestant Reformation in England.[103] The Bible translator Miles Coverdale "was ordained a priest, but as he studied the Scriptures he soon realized the error of the Roman Catholic church and became a Reformation preacher."[104]

Students read nine pages of John Foxe's *Book of Martyrs* so that they may meditate on Catholic persecution and cruelty. They also read John Milton's "On the Late Massacre in Piedmont," a thundering attack on the Catholic oppression of the Waldensians. Milton calls the pope "a triple tyrant," identifies the Catholic Church with the Biblical Babylon, and pleads that

God will "avenge thy slaughtered saints."[105]   Catholic martyrs for their convictions, however, are called traitors to England. They died, we are advised, for political, not religious, reasons. Therefore, about the poet Robert Southwell, we read, "By preaching Roman doctrine in England, he was guilty of treason and was imprisoned, tortured, and finally hanged."[106]   Anyone who knows anything about the executions of Southwell, Edmund Campion and others knows that they were put to death because they were priests and because the refused to renounce, under torture and unbelievable cruelty, such doctrines as Transubstantiation and papal primacy.   They have as much right to be called martyrs as do Latimer and Ridley, but students who absorb this volume will only remember the Catholic martyrs as traitors who got what they deserved.

John Foxe's *Book of Martyrs* is a particular favorite of these authors.   One text regales its readers with sixteen pages from this quintessential diatribe of the Reformation. While most historians regard Foxe's history as dubious, and as religious propaganda masquerading as history, this text presents it as both serious history and admirable literature. Foxe's book, it is said, "so engraved on the minds of his countrymen the cruelty of Catholic oppression that England since Foxe's time has never seriously been tempted to return to the Roman church."[107] Foxe "demonstrated that Protestantism, not papism, is primitive Christianity."[108]   It is conceded that "Foxe intends his accounts of the martyrs to show the genuineness of Protestant belief and the falseness of Catholic belief."[109]   The text also admits that "the book contains some factual inconsistencies."[110]   But Foxe's book is regarded as valuable because "it helped England remain Protestant when Romanism again threatened in the seventeenth century."[111]

The student's notes for Foxe reinforce religious distinctiveness.   The pope is labeled "Christ's enemy and antichrist."[112]   The word "papistical" is said to be a synonym for Catholic[113] while the term "Catholic" in the Apostle's Creed really means "universal Christian."[114]

All of the remaining authors selected for reading are Protestant. Except for Ben Jonson, none of the Catholic poets is included. Sir Philip Sydney's poetry is praised because it is "deeply tinged with the values of the Protestant Reformation."[115] Sir Walter Raleigh's "Even Such a Time" is referred to as "a moving declaration of Christian faith."[116]

William Shakespeare's works are given a decidedly Protestant Christian interpretation. The text claims that they "affirm the possibility of goodness and happiness as man acts in accordance with the will of God."[117] The judgmental tone pervading the Bob Jones University series can be seen in this passage. "We cannot say for certain that Shakespeare was personally a Christian. He was capable of some very low humor, even in plays whose moral tone is exceptionally high. We can say that intellectually Shakespeare was Christian. On moral and spiritual issues he thought as one whose convictions have been formed by the Word of God."[118] Since Shakespeare is "safe," students can read him with some discernment and profit.

A modern literature text presents a similar outlook. About King Charles II we read, "The new king, like his father, was unfriendly to Puritans and alarmingly agreeable to Catholic influences at court. His shameless immorality was a reproach to the nation. His brother, succeeding him as James II, displayed even more openly his Catholicism and moral looseness. He also stepped up the persecution of nonconforming Protestants . . ."[119] Therefore, "Many Englishmen began to fear the establishment of a Catholic dynasty."[120]

This text also adores John Foxe. "When English Protestantism was threatened with extinction during the reign of the Catholic Mary I, John Foxe undertook to chronicle the evils of Catholicism from earliest times to the present, demonstrating that Protestantism, not papism, was primitive Christianity. His *Acts and Monuments* (or *Book of Martyrs* as it is popularly called) kept Reformation zeal at a high pitch during the reign of Elizabeth I.[121] Soon thereafter, "The reigns of James I and the succeeding Stuart kings saw a drift toward Catholicism and rationalism among the clergy and in the royal patronage of the church."[122]

The intermingling of history and literature to attack Catholicism is common. Stuart England is depicted as a place where evil Papists were everywhere threatening to destroy Protestant England. "The near success of the Gunpowder Plot in 1605, in which thirteen Catholics conspired to blow up the Parliament building while Parliament, with the king in attendance, was in session, was horrifying proof of the reality of the Catholic threat to Protestant England."[123]   However, "The Catholic threat was averted by the accession of a Protestant queen."[124]   "In James II, Catholicism and moral libertinism were less guarded and more defiant than in Charles II, his brother.   James, the first avowed Catholic ruler since Bloody Mary, was arrogant, bigoted, and debauched."[125]   (It is interesting how often Catholic faith and sinful, depraved lifestyles are seen as synonymous.)   Here is another interpretation of the Stuart days. "James I was no Catholic, but his wife, Anne of Denmark, became a convert to Romanism.   In fact, all four Stuart kings had Catholic mothers and wives.   At the end of Elizabeth's reign, Romanists evidently realized they had a foothold at court making safe their return; the number of priests in England probably doubled with the accession of James. During the reign of Charles I, who patronized Catholic courtiers, conversions to Catholicism increased among High Anglican clergy and leading nobles, and Archbishop Laud steered the church in a Catholic direction. After 1660, royal friendliness to Catholicism became increasingly apparent, and the English feared a return of Catholic persecution."[126]

The relevance of these constant religious diatribes to the study of literature is never explained, though one clue is revealed in this comment. "Whereas Tudor poets drew abundantly from both medieval and classical traditions, their work remained fundamentally Protestant. Lyric poems of the next age were much more likely to take on a Catholic or pagan tone."[127] Catholic poetry is called "bizarre and sensuous."[128]

Little reminders of the evils of Popery appear everywhere. The Catholic Church concentrates on "undoing the work of the Protestant Reformation."[129] And, "Through its influence in politics and the media, modern Roman Catholicism has become, in fact, the nation's most powerful religious force."[130] Catholics are said to have "poured into the country from Mediterranean countries."[131]

Horton refers to Jesuits as "a hellish conclave" in a discussion of John Donne.[132] Anderson and Hicks say that the character Arthur Dimmesdale in *The Scarlet Letter* "shows that certain Roman Catholic practices regarding sin and guilt are to no avail."[133] St. John says that "During the period of domination by the Catholic Church, the Christian faith had become encumbered with multitudes of traditions, corrupting changes and human assumptions."[134]

Even attempts at fairness toward Catholic writers in Horton's modern British literature text fall far short of the goal. Five Roman Catholic writers are discussed: John Dryden, John Henry Newman, G. K. Chesterton, Gerard Manley Hopkins, and Francis Thompson.

But even in this apparent attempt at recognizing that many great English writers have been Catholic, the author finds it necessary to warn students that the religion itself is still unacceptable. For example, the section on Francis Thompson says, "Despite . . . the errors of the religious system with which he remained affiliated, Thompson sensed the presence of God in the world. We need not accept the genuineness of his religious experience to appreciate the truth and power of his claims for divine love."[135]

The selections chosen reveal religious bias. Nothing can ever be shown that depicts the Catholic understanding of faith favorably. Therefore the selections are mostly irrelevant and second-rate. They do not recognize the genius of the authors' work. It is arguable, for example, that conversion to Catholicism was the energizing principle which shaped and animated the major writing of Chesterton, Newman and Hopkins.

Chesterton's *Orthodoxy* and *The Everlasting Man* are considered among the finest, most lucid and most universally read discussions of religious faith ever written. They are also considered masterpieces of the expository essay writing genre. (C. S. Lewis once called *The Everlasting Man* the finest example of Christian apologetic in the English language.) Chesterton's Father Brown mystery stories are also highly appropriate for high school reading, showing as they do the application of logic and paradox to the solving of mysterious events. But the only Chesterton selections in this book are a few minor paragraphs about Dickens, which in no way reveal the range or depth of Chesterton's contributions as a writer. The student is short-changed and bored, and is not encouraged to seek out additional books by this masterful and quintessentially English author.

John Henry Newman's *Apologia* is a masterpiece of intellectual autobiography, and his *Idea of a University* is well regarded. But this text reproduces an obscure selection from *The Tamworth Reading Room*, written when Newman was a young Anglican cleric and essentially irrelevant to his later development as a mature writer and prose stylist. Newman scholars would be aghast.

Religious bias also permeates the historical background to the literary selections and the biographical sketches of those writers selected. The author is particularly careful to warn students that Newman and Hopkins still had "spiritual struggles and dark questioning"[136] after their conversion to Catholicism. He seems to think that all doubts and struggles vanish overnight after religious conversion, a naive and simplistic view that belies reality. Students are also told that "After his [Chesterton's] conversion to Roman Catholicism in 1922, his writing became more religiously partisan."[137]

A science text claims that the "educated" church leaders deliberately kept "the ignorant in submission with tales and threats."[138] Thomas Aquinas "often misrepresented Aristotle and even occasionally contradicted the Bible."[139]   Students are also told, "In Catholic dogma, prohibiting the laity from reading the Scripture because they would misinterpret it made good political sense. Keep the peasants ignorant, and they will believe anything they are told. It is only within the last 100 years that Catholics have been permitted to read the Bible."[140]   The text fails to differentiate between the clergy and members of religious orders, who were permitted to read and study the Scriptures, and the laity, who generally did not do so.

In its treatment of Latin America, an anti-Catholic perspective pervades a major geography text. We are told that "the people of Central America need more than money: they need to hear the message of the gospel. Most people are Roman Catholic by religion, and it was not until the 1900s that Protestant missionaries began to take the story of Jesus Christ to the Central Americans. There are still many people who have not heard how to be saved."[141]   For the Caribbean region, the reader is advised: "Since the days of Spanish rule, the majority of the people on many of the islands have been Roman Catholics. Often Catholicism is combined with voodooism and idol worship imported from Africa. The West Indies also has an impressive history of Protestant witness, however. Some of the first missionaries of modern times went there, and many Christians in the West Indies have endured great hardship to maintain a good Christian testimony."[142]

The section on South America is critical of the religious traditions of that continent. The author writes:

"Before the Europeans came to Latin America, the Indians worshiped anything they could not understand—the sun, the moon, animals, trees, and water. The Spanish and Portuguese explorers were accompanied by Catholic priests who converted many Indians to Catholicism, often at the point of a sword. For many centuries, the Bible in South America has been almost an unknown book. The Indians often accepted the outward form of Catholicism and combined it with their own pagan worship.

"Today, over 90 percent of all Latin Americans are Roman Catholics. The Catholic churches are huge, lavishly furnished buildings that contrast greatly with the poor houses of most of the people. One of the world's most expensive church buildings is in Salvador, Brazil's oldest city. The church auditorium is covered with pure gold."[143]

However, Protestant missionaries are seen as potential saviors to the region since they bring enlightenment and truth to that benighted continent.

"The First Protestant missionary to South America, an Englishman named James Thomson, did not arrive until 1820. He started schools in Argentina, Uruguay, Chile, and Peru. The Bible was the main textbook. Thomson's schools were received warmly at first but were later persecuted by Catholic officials.

Other missionaries went through great hardships to get the Bible into the South American countries. One Argentinian Christian, Francisco Penzotti, went to Paraguay as a missionary, where he was imprisoned for selling Bibles.

"South Americans who accepted Christ faced persecution from their friends and neighbors, but many stood firm in their new faith. By 1900, there was a Protestant witness in every country of South America."[144]

NOTES

1. David A. Fisher, *World History for Christian Schools* (Greenville, SC: Bob Jones University Press, 1984), p. 116.
2. *Ibid.*, p. 116.
3. *Ibid.*, pp. 179-180.
4. *Ibid.*, p. 181.
5. *Ibid.*, p. 182.
6. *Ibid.*, p. 185.
7. *Ibid.*, p. 182.
8. *Ibid.*, p. 185.
9. *Ibid.*, p. 180.
10. *Ibid.*, p. 182.

11. *Ibid.*, p. 181.

12. *Ibid.*, p. 183.

13. *Ibid.*, p. 181.

14. *Ibid.*, pp. 182-183.

15. *Ibid.*, p. 184.

16. *Ibid.*, p. 183.

17. *Ibid.*, p. 185.

18. *Ibid.*, p. 180.

19. *Ibid.*, p. 180.

20. *Ibid.*, p. 191.

21. *Ibid.*, p. 203.

22. *Ibid.*, p. 203.

23. *Ibid.*, p. 203.

24. *Ibid.*, p. 204.

25. *Ibid.*, p. 207.

26. *Ibid.*, p. 205.

27. *Ibid.*, p. 207.

28. *Ibid.*, p. 222.

29. *Ibid.*, pp. 246-248.

30. *Ibid.*, p. 242.

31. *Ibid.*, p. 243.

32. *Ibid.*, p. 243.

33. Glen Chambers and Gene Fisher, *United States History for Christian Schools* (Greenville, SC: Bob Jones University Press, 1982), p.15.

34. *Ibid.*, p. 16.

35. *Ibid.*, pp. 16-17.

36. *Ibid.*, p. 18.

37. *Ibid.*, p. 18.

38. *Ibid.*, p. 18.

39. *Ibid.*, pp. 18-19.

40. *Ibid.*, p. 19.

41. *Ibid.*, p. 19.

42. *Ibid.*, p. 20.

43. *Ibid.*, p. 20.

44. *Ibid.*, p. 20.

45. *Ibid.*, p. 22.
46. *Ibid.*, p. 21.
47. *Ibid.*, pp. 25-26.
48. *Ibid.*, p. 29.
49. *Ibid.*, p. 29.
50. *Ibid.*, p. 35.
51. *Ibid.*, p. 41.
52. *Ibid.*, p.73
53. *Ibid.*, p. 73.
54. *Ibid.*, p. 73.
55. *Ibid.*, p. 97.
56. *Ibid.*, p. 116.
57. *Ibid.*, p. 455.
58. *Ibid.*, p. 92.
59. *Ibid.*, p. 92.
60. *Ibid.*, p. 92.
61. *Ibid.*, p. 104.
62. *Ibid.*, p. 284.
63. *Ibid.*, p. 46.
64. *Ibid.*, p. 50.
65. *Ibid.*, p. 93.
66. *Ibid.*, p. 349.
67. *Ibid.*, p. 349.
68. *Ibid.*, p. 349.
69. *Ibid.*, p. 277.
70. *Ibid.*, p. 442.
71. Michael R. Lowman, *United States History in Christian Perspective* (Pensacola, FL: Pensacola Christian College, 1983), p. 468.
72. *Ibid.*, p. 13.
73. *Ibid.*, p. 13.
74. *Ibid.*, p. 3.
75. *Ibid.*, p. 3.
76. Ronald A. Horton, *British Literature for Christian Schools: The Early Tradition, 700-1688* (Greenville, SC: Bob Jones University Press, 1980), p. 7.

77. *Ibid.*, p. 6.
78. *Ibid.*, p. 12.
79. *Ibid.*, p. 12.
80. *Ibid.*, p. 15.
81. *Ibid.*, p. 15.
82. *Ibid.*, p. 62.
83. *Ibid.*, p. 63.
84. *Ibid.*, p. 74.
85. *Ibid.*, p. 68.
86. *Ibid.*, p. 126.
87. *The Holy Day Book*, (New York, NY: Harcourt, Brace, 1956), p. 70.
88. *The Church's Year*, (New York, NY: Oxford University Press, 1950),   p. 222.
89. Horton, p. 133.
90. *Ibid.*, p. 145.
91. *Ibid.*, p. 150.
92. *Ibid.*, p. 160.
93. *Ibid.*, p. 163
94. *Ibid.*, p. 164.
95. *Ibid.*, p. 164.
96. *Ibid.*, p. 164.
97. *Ibid.*, p. 180.
98. *Ibid.*, p. 181.
99. Jan Anderson and Laurel Hicks, *Introduction to English Literature, Classics for Christians, Vol. 5* (Pensacola, FL: Pensacola Christian College, A Beka Book Publication, 1982), p. 14.
100. *Ibid.*, p. 24.
101. *Ibid.*, p. 54
102. *Ibid.*, p. 47.
103. *Ibid.*, p. 81.
104. *Ibid.*, p. 89.
105. *Ibid.*, p. 244.
106. *Ibid.*, p. 119.
107. Horton, p. 197.

108. *Ibid.*, p. 200.
109. *Ibid.*, p. 201.
110. *Ibid.*, p. 201.
111. *Ibid.*, p. 202.
112. *Ibid.*, p. 211.
113. *Ibid.*, p. 211.
114. *Ibid.*, p. 211.
115. *Ibid.*, p. 225.
116. *Ibid.*, p. 235.
117. *Ibid.*, p. 267.
118. *Ibid.*, p. 268.
119. Ronald A. Horton, *British Literature for Christian Schools: The Modern Tradition, 1688 to the Present* (Greenville, SC: Bob Jones University Press, 1982), p. 3.
120. *Ibid.*, p. 3.
121. *Ibid.*, pp. 8-9.
122. *Ibid.*, p. 9.
123. Horton, *British Literature: The Modern Tradition*, pp. 289-290.
124. *Ibid.*, p. 294.
125. *Ibid.*, p. 293.
126. *Ibid.*, p. 296.
127. *Ibid.*, p. 299.
128. *Ibid.*, p. 299.
129. Raymond A. St. John, *American Literature for Christian Schools, Book 2, (Realism, Naturalism, and Modern American Literature,*Teacher's Edition (Greenville, SC: Bob Jones University Press, 1991), p. 540.
130. *Ibid.*, p. 541.
131. *Ibid.*, p. 540.
132. Horton, p. 315.
133. Jan Anderson and Laurel Hicks, *Beginnings of American Literature, Classics for Christians, Vol. 3*, (Pensacola, FL: Pensacola Christian College, A Beka Book Publication, 1982), p. 327.
134. St. John, Book 1, pp. 126-127.

135. Horton, *British Literature, The Modern Tradition*, p. 346.

136. *Ibid.*, p. 342.

137. *Ibid.*, p. 351.

138. William S. Pinkston, Jr., *Biology for Christian Schools, Book 1*, Teacher's Edition Greenville, SC: Bob Jones University Press, 1991), p. 649.

139. *Ibid.*, p. 649.

140. *Ibid.*, p. 649.

141. Laurel Elizabeth Hicks, *New World History and Geography in Christian Perspective* (Pensacola, FL: Pensacola Christian College, 1982), p. 140.

142. *Ibid.*, p. 155.

143. *Ibid.*, p. 176.

144. *Ibid.*, p. 177.

3

PITY THE POOR DEMOCRATS

Those who study American history in fundamentalist schools receive a novel view of our nation's political development. They are told that every Democratic president departed from constitutional principles of limited government, instead preferring to advance the behemoth of the secular state and a socialist economic system.   Even those presidents universally regarded by historians as great or near great receive short shrift in the texts prepared for the fast-growing fundamentalist school movement in the United States. Consider Franklin Roosevelt.

FDR, still an admired and beloved figure to average Americans and historians alike, is labeled a failure in texts used in most conservative Protestant schools.   One text says, "In retrospect, the New Deal, as Roosevelt's programs were called, did more harm than good. . . . Roosevelt's policies, which were often ill-planned and experimental, increased government spending and the power of the federal bureaucracy."[1]

A civics book reiterates this theme. "The New Deal was giving the federal government wide powers over industry and commerce, areas that were not government's rightful sphere.

Roosevelt's agencies were replacing the free enterprises of capitalism with the government regulations of socialism."[2]

A U.S. history text tells students: Franklin Roosevelt's "campaign rhetoric proved irresistible"[3] to American voters and his "new Deal policies substituted economic security for economic freedom."[4] In addition, "Many Americans have said that under the New Deal, the American people took a large step away from a constitutional republic based upon law toward a socialist democracy based upon total 'equality' for the masses."[5]

Another U.S. history book, published by Bob Jones University Press, is even harsher. "Religious liberals of the time scoffed at the gospel and declared that the only important things were the fatherhood of God and the brotherhood of man. Wallace and the other New Dealers went further; they declared, in effect, that even the fatherhood of God was unimportant and that only the brotherhood of man mattered."[6] The authors also mention, completely without relevance, that Eleanor and Franklin Roosevelt "had ceased to be personally close by 1920."[7] The only good thing said about FDR was that he "had become a legend."[8]

The Bob Jones University book continues to portray postwar America in a way calculated to create contempt in readers for the Democratic Party and liberal policies.

Harry Truman's Fair Deal "proposed a more thorough welfare state than that already established by the New Deal."[9] Henry Wallace's Progressives "were an assortment of Communists, pacifists, ex-New Dealers, and sincere but deluded liberals. Their nominee, Henry A. Wallace, campaigned for peace with the Soviets at any price."[10]

Senator Joseph R. McCarthy is treated favorably. His cause is seen as essentially just but flawed by his behavior. "Many of his accusations were indeed true . . . The liberal media soon discredited him. . . . his behavior did considerable damage to his good cause."[11]

The Warren Supreme Court "attempted to remold society."[12] The *Brown v. Board of Education* decision outlawing school segregation was "based . . . not mainly on legal precedent . . . but instead on the testimony of sociological experts."[13] And the High Court "had imposed further federal control on locally controlled school systems."[14]

The United Nations is denounced as "unbiblical"[15]. . .its aim of eventual one-world government goes directly against the plan of God, Who dispersed the nations at the tower of Babel when they sought to unify (Genesis 11:6-8)."[16]

The treatment of President John F. Kennedy is insulting, sarcastic, skewed by anti-Catholic prejudice. "Kennedy's convincing and charming television manner increased his popularity considerably. Throughout the campaign his Roman Catholicism, like Smith's in 1928, naturally became an issue. Many voters, distrusting the political influence of the Roman Catholic church, distrusted Kennedy as well. Many Catholics, on the other hand, supported him simply because he was Catholic."[17] Not a word is said about Kennedy's Houston speech pledging unequivocal support for separation of church and state. The text then stops just short of accusing the Democrats of stealing the 1960 election, which is called "so close that the Republicans accused the Democrats of foul play. Though the charge was never proved, the election results made it clear that Kennedy's victory was not a mandate for change."[18]

Even JFK's death is treated with sarcasm. "His popularity had been declining rapidly. Civil rights leaders were not satisfied with his support of their programs; liberal leaders sought greater federal spending; conservative leaders were especially concerned by his failures in foreign affairs. Yet after his assassination, he became the virtual hero of the age."[19]

The treatment of the 1964 election is clearly pro-Goldwater. "The Republicans nominated Arizona's Senator Barry Goldwater, a firm conservative who denounced the Social Security system, federal income tax, civil rights legislation, and other government actions that enlarged the federal bureaucracy.

He favored dealing firmly with Communist aggression in Vietnam and using American technology to oppose Communism.

"Goldwater fought a losing battle from the beginning. Besides representing a minority party, he frightened many voters by his indiscreet statements—some of which were magnified by an antagonistic press—about how he would conduct the war in Vietnam. Further, Johnson's warm, charming manner gained the confidence of many Americans who based their political support on personality rather than on issues."[20] President Lyndon Johnson is also called "politically unscrupulous and unprincipled."[21]

America in the 1960s is seen as a vile place. "America was seeing in its youth the product of the godless, materialistic society it had become. Since World War II the public schools had become secular. The theory of evolution had reduced man to the status of a mere animal. Permissiveness in behavior, including sexual behavior, was encouraged. Duty to God was replaced by duty to society. Without any real reason to maintain high moral and ethical standards, the youth threw off all restraint."[22]

The 1968 Democratic Convention riots are blamed solely on the peace demonstrators, though an independent commission called it a "police riot." "Outside the convention hall, members of the Youth International party and other radical groups, mainly protesting Humphrey's Vietnam policies, harassed police and National Guardsmen who had been called in to keep order. The demonstrators threw beverage cans and garbage at the authorities while shouting obscenities and leftist slogans. Police officers used force to disperse the crowd. Hundreds were injured, though none were killed. Radicals used the fact that some innocent spectators were victims of police violence to gain sympathy for their cause."[23]

George Wallace's 1968 campaign is treated sympathetically. "Wallace favored firmly crushing revolutionary demonstrations, waging a purposeful war in Vietnam, and increasing local and individual freedom. . . . Wallace's third-party effort was historically significant. He won nearly 10 million popular votes—more than any other third-party candidate in history—and carried five southern states."[24]   Wallace's showing was actually less significant as a percentage of the popular vote than that of LaFollette in 1924 or Roosevelt in 1912.

The Kent State upheaval in 1970 is portrayed this way: "During May 1970 a rock-throwing mob at Ohio's Kent State University either angered or frightened National Guardsmen into firing at them. Four young people were killed and several others injured in what the press called the 'Kent State Massacre.'"[25] The Pentagon Papers "revealed the blunders and deceptions of the Kennedy and Johnson administrations in the conduct of the Vietnam conflict."[26]

The Vietnam War is praised and the United States defeat is blamed on the liberal media. "Limitations placed on U.S. military personnel by their own government, held virtually hostage by a hostile press and the constant threat of riots, made winning the war impossible."[27]

Nixon is criticized for lying during Watergate and because he and "many of his advisers were shockingly foul-mouthed."[28]   But according to the author, the press deserves more blame. "Perhaps the most important cause of the unusual outcry over Watergate was the power of the press. . . . The public fell victim to this manipulation, in essence living at the mercy of the most influential typewriter. Another cause was Nixon's own ineptitude and unrepentant spirit. . . . he looked, spoke, and acted like a criminal, provoking the bloodthirsty press and alienating the suspicious public."[29]

Jimmy Carter is seen as "a weak and ineffective president"[30] whose "programs proved ineffective . . . because he was not spending enough to satisfy minorities or labor."[31]

Ronald Reagan came to America's rescue. "He was an energetic and charming candidate. A strong conservative, he called for a stronger military, lower taxes, and a balanced budget. Several issues in 1980 were of particular importance to

Christians."[32] Among these were the Equal Rights Amendment, abortion, homosexuality, and government regulation of religious schools. "During the campaign Reagan's views on all these issues were decidedly more acceptable to Bible-believing Christians than were Carter's.[33] The Christian vote was decisive. "Largely because of the support of the so-called 'New Right,' a renewed conservative and Christian political activism, Reagan won in an electoral landslide, 489 to 49. . ."[34]

The text ends with a selection from Reagan's First Inaugural.

A Pensacola Christian College Press text reveals a similar point of view.

John F. Kennedy was elected only because his "good looks, polish and charisma won the television audience."[35] Barry Goldwater was the preferred choice of this book in its explanation of the 1964 election. "Goldwater stated his opposition to the mushrooming federal bureaucracy and the burgeoning welfarism of the Johnson administration and urged a return to a Constitutional system of limited government."[36]

FBI Director J. Edgar Hoover is praised because he "understood the importance of maintaining America's traditional moral values."[37] Senator Joseph McCarthy's "investigations then, and later, indicated that a large number of left-wing, pro-Soviet liberals—if not outright Communists—had worked their way into the federal government."[38] Even though "McCarthy's personality and his conduct before television cameras did not give him a good public image. . . . the essence of what he said was never disproved or denied."[39]

A junior high school civics text conveys an admiration for Ronald Reagan. Republicans are clearly preferred in the text. Ronald Reagan's speeches were "direct, sincere and stirring."[40] Here is the background to the Reagan presidency. ". . . the failures in both domestic and foreign policy during the Ford and Carter years had given the whole nation a sense of weakness and an inability to deal with problems. Ronald Reagan offered to restore American strength and pride, and the people were once again willing for their leader to take charge of affairs."[41]

All efforts to bring about world peace are ridiculed by these authors because "lasting peace on earth will be possibly only when the Lord Jesus Christ returns," according to a widely-used world history text.[42] The same text reviles the United Nations. "World leaders have vainly sought global unity through organizations like the United Nations. Throughout history man has unsuccessfully striven for manmade, one-world government. The fall of many empires over the centuries illustrates that human unity that denies God cannot succeed. God judges all attempts at one-world government, just as He condemned the building of the Tower of Babel. . ."[43]

President Kennedy's Peace Corps is also dismissed as worthless. "Much of the work of the Peace Corps was good, but it met only a few of the temporal needs of the people the Corps intended to help. Its work provided no permanent solutions for the world's needs.   Christians should realize that although helping the poor and needy is good, people have a spiritual need that only the Lord Jesus can satisfy,"[44] says one book. Another text calls it "less than successful."[45]

Dr. Martin Luther King's work on behalf of civil rights and social justice meets with criticism. One book opines that King's "techniques sometimes resulted in violence."[46]   Also, "Instead of preaching the gospel, however, he spoke of liberating the poor and underprivileged peoples from their misery through social action."[47] The Bob Jones University text contributes this opinion: "Racial strife, which had been only moderate after the extreme outbreaks of the late 1960s, broke out again. The inflammatory issue this time was busing to achieve racial balance—forcing schoolchildren to go across town to school so that all schools in a district could have similar racial distributions."[48]

These texts have no use for labor unions. The Bob Jones University text is quite emphatic.

Labor unions are rarely praised for trying to improve working conditions, safety, health care, or wages for America's working people. Instead, the violence of strikes is repeatedly emphasized, and unions are blamed for rising prices to consumers and lack of interest in nonunion workers."[49] Hoping to improve their income and working conditions, labor leaders renewed efforts to organize labor during the twenties. These efforts frequently resulted in strikes. Throughout the summer of 1922, coal miners across the nation were on strike. In June, strikers in Illinois shot and killed twenty nonunion mineworkers and wounded several others for not participating in the strike."[50] Also, "Those in the labor movement were irritated by the lavish spending of the wealthy; Marxist agitation encouraged further discontent."[51] Students are told, "The main cause of man's dissatisfaction is failure to receive as much as he expects."[52]

During the Depression, "Labor became yet another avenue for government spending and control. The unemployment caused by the depression intensified labor conflicts throughout the thirties. There were many fairly small but sometimes violent strikes in the textile, auto, and steel industries."[53] Furthermore, "Labor unions had been creating turmoil in American industry since the war,"[54] and "large unions have become increasingly vulnerable to graft and corruption."[55] Union members "went from door to door" campaigning for Roosevelt in 1944, "reminding voters of the depression and suggesting that it had been the fault of the Republican Party."[56]

Unions are castigated for their "failure to govern the greed of their members."[57] Nothing is said about the greed of corporate interests or the lack of concern of employers for the well being of their employees.

Students are also told bluntly, "Most of the major labor strikes in our history have been immoral."[58]

This text also reiterates the value of conservative, free enterprise economic systems. In a section on economic principles we read, "1. God is the Creator of all resources. 2. God has appointed man steward of Creation. . . . 3. Because of man's sin, God has decreed that he must either labor or starve."[59]

Communal living "failed at Jamestown and Plymouth . . . because it rejects basic biblical teachings."[60] "It was the biblical thinking of most of the colonists . . . that made the principle of private property important in colonial America . . ."[61]

Hard work is ordained by God. "Most Americans believed that it was their duty before God to work hard and to be productive. They believed, as did the Puritans, that this was the scriptural formula for success."[62]

Little is said about social justice or compassion on the part of government in the economic realm. Nor are there any biblical citations from Old Testament prophets who castigated the selfish and greedy rich of their times. Jesus's reflection that "the love of money is the root of all evil" is nowhere to be found in this supposedly Bible-centered textbook.

Another text repeatedly praises the "moral values of Capitalism,"[63] including a full-page defense of capitalism written by a Massachusetts bishop in 1901. "Free enterprise capitalism is the only economic system capable of providing the greatest material benefits for the greatest number of people."[64] American financiers are praised for their generosity to Christian enterprises. "Financially successful businessmen in the Age of Industry gave large amounts of money to support various denominational efforts and other Christian endeavors. Many of these entrepreneurs were staunch church members."[65]   J. Pierpont Morgan is portrayed as "a generous philanthropist" who "supported Christian endeavors."[66]

The Larson-Creason volume for junior high school students reviles government efforts to help the poor, who are seen as largely responsible for their own plight.

The text sneers continually at government help to the poor. "Some of this government aid has helped a few who were in need, but it cannot wipe out poverty. . . . We can look throughout history and see that there has always been some poverty."[67] Therefore, "It becomes easier for those who want aid for whatever reason to cry to the government for help. Also, it relieves Americans of the responsibility and blessing of helping those who are truly in need."[68] This point is reiterated in the chapter on the New Deal. "Too few, however, learned to fully trust in God in the midst of their hardships. It was easier to ask the government for aid."[69]

Fatalism pervades the text. There is little or nothing individuals can do to solve problems except to convert the poor to fundamentalism. "In this world little can be done to solve problems for the entire nation,"[70] the text opines. Christians should help the "deserving" poor but should be careful of unbelievers. "Christians do have a responsibility to help the poor, but they also have a responsibility to be good stewards of what money they have. Therefore, they should be careful that any money they contribute for the needy goes for worthy causes. It should not be allowed to support sinful practices of the needy, and it should not fill the pockets of the administrators of undeserving charitable organizations or support organizations that are antagonistic to the Gospel."[71]

This dislike of Democratic and liberal policies is reinforced by a preference for Republican presidencies, particularly those which are also suffused with evangelical religion. The Pensacola Christian College text for U.S. history reveals this preference in several passages.

The late nineteenth century Republican presidents are seen as noble and virtuous. "Fortunately for the nation, however, the men who occupied the White House during the latter half of the nineteenth century were of notably high character and integrity. Many held deep religious convictions."[72] President Ulysses Grant, a notorious drunkard whose administration was grossly corrupt, is quoted as calling the Bible "The sheet-anchor of our liberties."[73] President Rutherford Hayes, whose election is regarded as stolen by many historians, is admired because his wife "refused to serve alcoholic beverages in the White House."[74]

President James Garfield's "defense of the Bible" takes up most of one page.[75] Benjamin Harrison "was an elder in the Presbyterian church for over forty years; he also served as a deacon and Sunday school teacher."[76] William McKinley "was a loyal member of the Methodist church, and throughout his long political career, his public life reflected his belief that Christianity is the mightiest factor in the civilization of the world. He was known for his abstinence from alcoholic beverages and his abhorrence of profanity and off-color stories."[77] The connection between Republicanism and evangelical piety is well established, at least in the mind of this book's author.

Herbert Hoover is praised as "a good example of the American self-made man"[78] while his 1928 Democratic opponent Al Smith merely "worked his way up through the ranks of New York City politics."[79] Mixing anti-Catholicism with Republican sympathy, the text describes the 1928 campaign this way: "At a time when the United States strongly favored Protestantism, when many citizens still favored prohibition, and when there was a strong emphasis on '100 percent Americanism,' Al Smith, a 'wet' Catholic of immigrant descent, was an unlikely candidate for the Presidency. Smith was also subject to criticism because of his political connections to Tammany Hall."[80]

Rutherford Hayes and James Garfield are admired by the Bob Jones University text. Certain Presidents known to be pious evangelicals are praised. Rutherford Hayes "had high ideals. His personal life was exemplary. He and his family prayed and read the Bible daily. Their firm convictions were characterized by Mrs. Hayes's refusal to serve alcohol in the White House."[81] Garfield "was a devoutly religious man and showed genuine respect for the Bible."[82] The unsuccessful Republican presidential candidate in 1884, James G. Blaine, is lauded because his "personal life was orderly and virtuous."[83]

Calvin Coolidge and Hayes appear favorably in a civics and government text. "Note that the economic problems brewing during the Coolidge administration were not the president's fault but rather the result of foolish money management on the part of millions of Americans."[84] Rutherford B. Hayes and his wife Lucy were "wholesome and God-fearing,"[85] who sang hymns in the Red Room and held family devotions and prayer in the Blue Room."[86]

A geography text also adores McKinley, Garfield, and Coolidge, largely for religious reasons. "William McKinley, the President of the United States, was a devout Christian who attended the Methodist church regularly. He took a courageous stand against liquor, swearing, and the telling of dirty stories, and he was known for his personal purity."[87]

Garfield, who was assassinated shortly after his inauguration, is admired because he was an evangelical believer and a lay preacher of the Disciples of Christ church. Two pages are devoted to Garfield, who is described as spiritual, gentle, well educated, and honest. Young Garfield, who had survived a boating accident, "knew God had saved his life for some purpose beyond that of being a canal hand."[88]

Calvin Coolidge is called "a man of good sense." The author extols this mediocre president in glowing terms: "He was known for his scholarship, character, frugality, quiet humor, and good sense. He understood the people of the United States. He knew their strengths and their weaknesses, and he often said that the strength of the nation depended upon the character of the people.

"President Coolidge, who was from New England, greatly admired his Puritan ancestors. He spent a great deal of time studying their history and writings, and he also became a student of the Bible. From the Puritans and the Bible he learned the character traits that made generations of Americans great."[89]

The only GOP President who is somewhat less than admired is the liberal Theodore Roosevelt, and even he is praised for his personal piety. The Bob Jones University text takes the Progressive Movement of the early twentieth century to task because "Sometimes progressivism took on the nature of a crusade and became a humanistic substitute for biblical Christianity."[90] But Democrat Woodrow Wilson is seen as a naive idealist, under whose "leadership, or lack of leadership, the United States lost her political balance."[91]

Returning to the 1990s, we see a hard right bias to these textbooks and their presentation of contemporary social and political problems. Abortion is seen as a despicable crime. The Bob Jones University world history text says, "The murder of unborn children, far surpassing Hitler's horrible extermination of several million Jews, has become socially acceptable."[92] The Larson-Creason volume calls abortion "legalized murder [which] destroys nearly one-third of all American babies each year."[93]

Larson and Creason continue in the same view as they explore other social issues. About the Equal Rights Amendment we are informed, "This amendment seemed harmless, but it would have given the government virtually unlimited power to interfere in women's lives. . . . Moreover, many feminists were seeking to erase the God-given differences between men and women. . . . Some even went so far as to attack marriage, support abortion, and advocate other immoral and unBiblical practices."[94]   The gay rights movement is labeled "despicable."[95]   These "immoral Americans not only try to excuse their sin as simply another choice of lifestyle but also try to demand special recognition and privilege."[96]   Changes in family life come from the Devil. "One of Satan's strongest attacks on America and on the church comes from his attacks on the family unit."[97] Indeed, America today is called "a society where God is commonly rejected."[98] Environmentalists are ridiculed as "pantheists who almost worship nature as a god."[99]

NOTES

1. David A. Fisher, *World History for Christian Schools* (Greenville, SC: Bob Jones University Press, 1984), pp. 548-49.

2. Rachel C. Larson with Pamela B. Creason, *The American Republic for Christian Schools* (Greenville, SC: Bob Jones University Press, 1988) p. 516.

3. Michael R. Lowman, *United States History in Christian Perspective* (Pensacola, FL: Pensacola Christian College, 1983), p. 530.

4. *Ibid.*, p. 531.

5. *Ibid.*, p. 532.

6. Glen Chambers and Gene Fisher, *United States History for Christian Schools* (Greenville, SC: Bob Jones University Press, 1982), p. 473.

7. *Ibid.*, p. 473.

8. *Ibid.*, p. 529.

9. *Ibid.*, p. 547.

10. *Ibid.*, p. 547.

11. *Ibid.*, p. 550.

12. *Ibid.*, p. 554.

13. *Ibid.*, p. 555.

14. *Ibid.*, p. 555.

15. *Ibid.*, p. 559.

16. *Ibid.*, p. 543.

17. *Ibid.*, p. 561.

18. *Ibid.*, p. 562.

19. *Ibid.*, p. 569.

20. *Ibid.*, p. 571.

21. *Ibid.*, p. 571.

22. *Ibid.*, pp. 575-76.

23. *Ibid.*, pp. 583-84.

24. *Ibid.*, p. 584.

25. *Ibid.*, p. 586.

26. *Ibid.*, p. 586.
27. *Ibid.*, p. 577.
28. *Ibid.*, p. 592.
29. *Ibid.*, p. 592.
30. *Ibid.*, p. 601.
31. *Ibid.*, p. 597.
32. *Ibid.*, p. 601.
33. *Ibid.*, p. 601.
34. *Ibid.*, p. 601.
35. Lowman, p. 586.
36. *Ibid.*, p. 593.
37. *Ibid.*, p. 492.
38. *Ibid.*, p. 567.
39. *Ibid.*, p. 567.
40. Larson and Creason, p. 586.
41. *Ibid.*, p. 587.
42. *Ibid.*, p. 542.
43. *Ibid.*, p. 607.
44. Larson and Creason, p. 566.
45. Chambers and Fisher, p. 565.
46. Larson and Creason, p. 572.
47. *Ibid.*, p. 572.
48. Chambers and Fisher, p. 594.
49. *Ibid.*, 370-371.
50. *Ibid.* p. 457.
51. *Ibid.*, p. 457.
52. *Ibid.*, p. 458.
53. *Ibid.*, p. 485.
54. *Ibid.*, p. 547.
55. *Ibid.*, p. 549.
56. *Ibid.*, p. 522.
57. *Ibid.*, p. 608.
58. *Ibid.*, p. 332.
59. *Ibid.*, p. 181.
60. *Ibid.*, p. 40.
61. *Ibid.*, p. 59.

62. *Ibid.*, p. 271.

63. Lowman, p. 360.

64. Lowman, p. 361.

65. Lowman, p. 361.

66. Lowman, p. 355.

67. Larson and Creason, p. 607.

68. *Ibid.*, p. 607.

69. *Ibid.*, p. 519.

70. *Ibid.*, p. 141 T.

71. *Ibid.*, p. 141T.

72. *Ibid.*, p. 403.

73. *Ibid.*, p. 404.

74. *Ibid.*, p. 405.

75. *Ibid.*, p. 406.

76. *Ibid.*, p. 409.

77. *Ibid.*, pp. 411-412.

78. *Ibid.*, p. 522.

79. *Ibid.*, p. 523.

80. *Ibid.*, p. 523.

81. Chambers and Fisher, p. 347.

82. *Ibid.*, p. 353.

83. *Ibid.*, p. 362.

84. Larson and Creason, p. 115T.

85. *Ibid.*, p. 370.

86. *Ibid.*, p. 370.

87. Laurel Elizabeth Hicks, *New World History and Geography in Christian Perspective* (Pensacola, FL: Pensacola Christian College, 1982), pp. 304, 305.

88. *Ibid.*, pp. 286-87.

89. *Ibid.*, p. 317.

90. Chambers and Fisher, p. 384.

91. *Ibid.*, p. 436.

92. *Ibid.*, p. 616.

93. Larson and Creason, p. 591.

94. *Ibid.*, p. 609.

95. *Ibid.*, p. 609.

96. *Ibid.*, p. 609.
97. *Ibid.*, p. 611.
98. *Ibid.*, p. 611.
99. *Ibid.*, p. 607.

4

A WRITER'S LOT IS NOT A HAPPY ONE

The literature books developed by the two primary publishers for fundamentalist schools have a decidedly negative view toward writers, American and British. With only a handful of exceptions, the most prominent authors in both heritages are roundly accused of despair, pessimism, and religious apostasy. The writers are routinely judged not by established literary criteria but by their adherence or nonadherence to conservative Protestant values.

The selection of essays, short stories, poems, novels and plays is skewed toward pious, didactic writings and frequently to mediocre writers who are deemed religiously safe. There is also a clear preference for Protestant writers, especially those of the Puritan and Victorian persuasions. Extravagant and nonscholarly assertions and generalizations abound in the texts.

A modern American literature text may be cited as representative.

The "modern writer typically does not hold anything to be absolute,"[1] "questions all philosophical and religious beliefs,"[2] and "has little respect for traditional literary forms."[3] "He rejects virtually all restrictions,"[4] and "tends to portray all actions no matter how vile and all words and thoughts no matter how crude or blasphemous."[5] "Having rebelled against Christianity and its promise of heaven or hell, writers lived only for the fleeting moment."[6] Writers also "rejected the past"[7] and "revolted against family and church, and against small-town life and its traditional values."[8] Some "made art their religion."[9] A few even rebelled "against life itself by choosing suicide as preferable to living."[10]

Even a U.S. history book manages to make the same point in its treatment of American writers of the 1920s. "The general pessimism of these writers probably reflected their own inadequacy as much as that of American society. They were confused men who could not decide whether to accept Victorian morality or Freudian psychology, capitalism or socialism. . . . Fitzgerald died prematurely because of heavy drinking and general dissipation. Hemingway committed suicide."[11]

Selectivity is the major factor in the quality of a literature textbook. The authors selected should be the major representatives of a nation's literary heritage. Certainly most of those included should be the examples generally agreed upon by specialists in the field. Secondly, the selections themselves should be representative of the author's output or *oeuvre*. Ideally, they should be among the best of the author's achievement.

There is nothing inherently wrong with including representatives of the religious tradition which sponsors the school, as long as those selections are generally reflective of good literature. Every ethnic and religious tradition has produced writers of some merit.

These volumes generally fail to achieve those objectives. Their primary deficiency comes from a particular religious slant which affects almost every biographical sketch and every passage of historical background. These volumes are suffused with sectarian emphases, interpretations and distortions.

As is true of the entire Bob Jones University series of textbooks, a newly published (1991) guide to American literature clearly prefers the Puritan experience in U.S. history and unreservedly denigrates the entire literary experience of the U.S. since independence.

The student is informed at the very beginning that, "The Puritans gave America not only a doctrinal system but also an idea of how life should be lived."[12] Furthermore, "they wished to establish a state governed by religious principles. They believed that their government should be theocratic (governed by God) rather than democratic (governed by the people). Since the Bible describes only one form of government specifically ordained by God, the theocratic government of Israel, the Puritans took it as their model."[13] There is a strong implication in this passage that theocracy is preferable to democracy.

We are told that Puritan theology "sought to complete the English Reformation by purifying the Church of England of all non-Scriptural elements retained from Roman Catholicism."[14]

Puritan writers are admired. "The legacy of the Puritan writers is an impressive one . . . for the Christian whose beliefs enable him to sympathize with Puritan experiences and goals. . . . It is a pleasure to begin the study of American literature with writings that teach what Christians have always believed."[15] Modern criticism of Puritan literature is dismissed. "Because Puritans deliberately cultivated a prose that was religious in content, didactic in purpose, and plain in style, their writing has suffered badly at the hands of critics who have preferred secular subject matter, ambiguity of purpose, and complexity of style."[16] The student reads carefully selected passages from William Bradford, John Winthrop, Mary Rowlandson, Samuel Sewell, Anne Bradstreet, Edward Taylor, and Jonathan Edwards, which comprise more than one-fourth of the text.

Jonathan Edwards is a particular favorite of the textbook's author because "The spiritual insight Edwards's work provides for a reader sympathetic to his experience and goals is unparalleled by that of any other American writer."[17] From Edwards's writings the student is supposed to learn "the Biblical truth that God's ways are not man's ways," and to "recognize the reality of the unconverted man's position before God."[18]

William Bradford's "life and writing reveal a Christian serving God in the confidence of His calling, willing to suffer in order to carry out what he believes to be God's will. His example encourages all Christians to rely on God's providential care."[19]

While Anglican writer William Byrd II is included, we are told that "his high-church Anglican background seems to keep religion somewhat at a distance from his personal life."[20]

Benjamin Franklin's writings, however, "clearly depict how far the nation had shifted from its Puritan foundation,"[21] primarily because his emphases "typify the new materialism becoming all too dominant in American life."[22] The text sneers at Franklin's religious views. "Franklin encouraged broad religious toleration. Because he held no personal beliefs, he was willing to accept any religion just as long as it made good citizens out of its converts. Although intimately acquainted with the evangelist George Whitefield, Franklin never admitted his own need for salvation."[23] Students are also told bluntly, "Franklin was never concerned with serving God or preparing for heaven."[24]

Thomas Paine is held in disrepute. "Paine's extreme rationalism and radical deism cost him his popularity, and he died in poverty and disfavor."[25] His career "is a reminder that great personal gifts can serve unworthy as well as worthy endeavors."[26] Paine is also accused of intellectual dishonesty. "The religious appeals carefully woven throughout his political writing were purposefully designed to influence an audience with conservative religious beliefs when Paine's own beliefs were, instead, radically Deistic."[27]

The teacher is instructed to attack Paine. "As you discuss Paine's arguments, compare them to modern liberal views. Point out to your students that modern attacks against God and His Word are fundamentally the same as Paine's."[28]

Paine's classic *Age of Reason* is called "shallow and naive"[29] and its arguments "have been tirelessly repeated by unbelievers up to the present."[30] Furthermore, "Paine's position anticipates modern religious liberalism, which is Unitarianism in Christian guise."[31]   But Paine's influence was "providentially hindered from having much immediate effect"[32] because it was "published during America's second major revival. . ."[33]

William Bartram's botanical diary "views God as an active and benevolent force in nature,"[34] but "nowhere does he reflect the Biblical view of God and nature expressed by the earliest American writers."[35]   Poet Philip Freneau's "view of the world is man-centered, for he replaces the providential, personal relationship of God with mankind with an impersonal and rationalistic divine benevolence."[36]   Poor Freneau.   His lack of true faith apparently affected his life.   "Freneau made increasingly frequent attempts to drown his unhappiness in liquor.   In 1832, when eighty years old, the poet died during a snowstorm while trying to find his way home at night from a tavern."[37]   In his writings "he omits any reference to man's need for salvation and to the atonement; he ignores God's providential care for his children."[38]

As American literature moved into the early nineteenth century and became influenced by individualism and Romanticism, a new degeneration is deplored.   "Nineteenth-century romanticism placed its faith in men. . . . As writers made romanticism their religion, they were shattered by the realization that the goodness of man was a mere phantom."[39]   Individualism is also denounced because it "contributed to the optimistic but naive notion that man is not a fallen creature, who in sinning has lost the ability to realize his potential.   The key Puritan doctrine of total depravity, a somber truth from the Bible, did not appeal to the romantic. . . . Thus, in their doctrine of the supremacy of the individual, the romantics were basically in rebellion against God's view of man."[40]

Virtually every outstanding writer included in this volume is labeled either as an enemy of Christianity or as defective in promoting Biblical truths and values.

William Cullen Bryant's poem, "Thanatopsis," "sounds a pagan call for resignation to death and denies the fact of an afterlife.   Because his religious views lack Biblical consistency, his poetry gives the uncertain sound against which Scripture warns us."[41]   Students are warned to "contrast Bryant's rationalistic view of death with the Christian viewpoint."[42]   The teacher is instructed to stress that, "Apart from God and the Truth of His Word, man has no knowledge of what lies beyond death.   His feeble attempts to find and give comfort fall sadly short of the mark."[43]   Washington Irving's works are criticized because their goal "was no longer moral or religious instruction but entertainment."[44]   John Greenleaf Whittier's poem about a Quaker worship service, "First-Day Thoughts," is "marred for the Christian reader by what it assumes to be true about the nature of man. . . .even though certain sentiments in the poem attract the Christian."[45]   Of Oliver Wendell Holmes it is said, "A scientific rationalist and outspoken Unitarian, Holmes sought to destroy the conservative religion of his fathers."[46]   Holmes's "The Chambered Nautilus" is criticized because he suggests "the possibility of man's improving his own 'soul,' which is an idealistic, humanistic premise."[47]

All of the poets of this era of romantic optimism are to be carefully examined.   The teacher is told, "The optimistic pronouncements that are often wedded to Biblical allusions . . . may cause students to accept the philosophy of the poets without careful thought.   Encourage them to read carefully, noting deviations from a Biblically sound philosophy of life. . . . For Christian readers they offer the challenge of separating Christian values from the idealistic, humanistic beliefs permeating their verse."[48]

James Fenimore Cooper receives mild praise, primarily because his character Natty Bumppo's "heroic greatness" was linked "to the Christian values taught him by Moravian missionaries."[49]   However, the teacher is instructed to caution students not to admire Native American religion. "Although there are some parts of Cooper's thought that violate Christian doctrine (e.g., that the Indian will go to his own happy hunting ground if he is true to the light God has given him, although the light is a lesser one than that given to the white man), his moral vision has its basis in Christian principles and ethics."[50]

American literature clearly begins its great slide downward with Emerson and Thoreau. The text begins with a denunciation of transcendentalism: "A rather awkward composite of philosophical bits and scraps, transcendentalism masqueraded as a religion . . . Fundamentally anti-Christian, the movement discarded the Bible, believing its truths relevant only to the original writers, not to present readers."[51] Students are told to "Refute the erroneous assumptions underlying transcendentalism," and "identify the erroneous ideas inherent in Emerson's writing."[52] Why is Ralph Waldo Emerson, so beloved by generations of American schoolteachers and students, so dangerous? Here is the answer. "From a Christian perspective this influence has been unwholesome. Emerson's doctrines of the divinity of man, the perfectibility of society, and the irrelevance of the Bible all attack the very basis of orthodox Christianity. It is no wonder, then, that Christians must repudiate the teachings both of Emerson and of his philosophical descendants."[53] Emerson's poem "Brahma" "reveals that the modern heresy which regards all gods as valid objects of worship and all religions as valid roads to heaven is nothing new."[54] Teachers are encouraged to "interpret each of Emerson's quotations and evaluate them in light of Scripture."[55]

Henry David Thoreau is seen as another wicked malcontent. "His assumptions and values demand the kind of careful scrutiny that only a Biblically grounded Christian can bring to an evaluation of its content. Thoreau conceives a world that begins and ends with self, denies the fact of man's corrupt nature, believes in salvation through self-achievement, and worships God only in nature. A hero to modern radicals, the father of twentieth-century primitivism, an anarchist seeking to pull down divinely instituted government, Thoreau is no model for the Christian."[56]

Thoreau's classic *Walden* is seen as destructive of the social, political and religious order. His ideal of self-reliance is "not derived from the Bible but from human egotism."[57] Asceticism and simplicity of life do not appeal to this textbook. "Practicing asceticism, or physical self-denial for spiritual advancement, is a pagan practice rather than a Christian one."[58] Thoreau is also denounced for "the inadequacy of his principles and his obvious deficiencies of character."[59]

Walt Whitman may be admired by many Americans but he is seen as "obnoxious"[60] and "blasphemous"[61] in this book. "With his own mind as his church, Whitman founded a new cult of self-worship, its tenets drawn from transcendentalism. . . . In extending Emerson's ideas to their logical outcome, Whitman illustrates the destructive effects of transcendentalism on the American mind. Understanding his contribution is necessary in our tracing a major current of degeneration in American literature and life."[62] We are informed that "the truths of the Bible evidently made no impact on him."[63] The teacher is told to stress that "a Christian's response to death differs from Whitman's."[64] Here is a sweeping summary of the life and work of "the good gray poet": "Whitman rejected the truth of God's Word, preferring the fabrication of man's reasoning to the eternal verities of the Bible."[65]

Sarcasm and negativism characterize the text's depiction of Edgar Allan Poe. He is "credited with being the father of the minor genre of the detective story."[66] Poe's work is summarized in this way: "Although Poe's perspective is not Biblically or even morally sound, his delineations of depraved men, twisted and tortured by their innermost natures, are in keeping with what we know of the effects of sin. . . . In terms of ethical significance, however, it is deficient, especially for the Christian reader."[67] Poe is also criticized for his alleged "preoccupation with the morbid side of man's nature."[68]

Nathaniel Hawthorne receives faint praise because "of all the American romantics, only Hawthorne expressed a viewpoint based on values sympathetic to those of Christianity."[69] However, he too, "evidently rejected the Puritan's faith in Christ and trust in the Bible."[70] In summary, "Although a religious skeptic, Hawthorne held the Biblical view of man as a flawed creature, unable to secure his own salvation or perfection. Hawthorne's fiction illustrates the truth that mankind's attempts to deny this moral reality produce only foolish pride and consequent failure."[71]

Herman Melville fares no better than most of the other authors of this era. In this section the text says that students should be able to "Recognize the pessimism in Melville's work," and, "Discern how Melville's rejection of God contributed to his pessimism."[72] We are told that "The dominant spirit of his writing is rebellion against God . . . Melville quarrels with God for having provided no meaning in the universe and virtually no hope of ultimate victory over the forces that oppose men. While his refutation of transcendentalism is valuable to the Christian, his refusal to accept the Biblical view of God and man mars his work. His writing is that of a searcher who, having turned away from the truth of God's Word, offers only questions, not answers."[73] The teacher's edition adds succinctly, "He rejects the whole truth of God's Word."[74]

The second volume in this publisher's American literature series continues these themes and patterns.

"Many writers of the late nineteenth century did not believe in God. They therefore pictured the world as controlled by nature or fate or blind chance."[75]

The literature of the era is said to reflect religious indifference. "American literature of the post-Civil War era virtually ignored the important theological controversy that produced fundamentalism. Late-nineteenth-century writers of serious fiction and poetry only occasionally touched on general religious issues. When they did, they tended to side with religious liberalism."[76] Even religious best-sellers are dismissed, as in this comment about Charles Sheldon's *In His Steps*: "What this novel unfortunately omits, like other religious best sellers of the age, is a clear-cut presentation of the gospel. It does not force readers to confront the reality of their sinful condition before God and their need for personal forgiveness of sin. "[77]

Most of the individual writers treated at length are condemned for their religious and philosophical points of view. Ambrose Bierce's "work reflects the strong undercurrent of bitterness in American writers at the turn of the century. The drift from the spiritual values of the earlier centuries was bringing only disillusionment. As man placed his faith in mankind rather than God, he was doomed to disappointment."[78] Bierce's writing "reflects the universal problem of someone's trying to establish values and discover life's meaning apart from God."[79] Sara Orne Jewett's "God seems little more than the romantic, pantheistic deity of Emerson and other New England writers of the nineteenth century. Her character studies, as a result, seldom reflect the reality of sin and guilt. . . ."[80]

Emily Dickinson "rebelled against God. As a result, her verse reveals the modern attitudes of doubt and denial."[81] The teacher is instructed to "compare Dickinson's definition of hope with the Biblical one."[82]

This theme of Dickinson's apostasy is reiterated. "Dickinson clearly rejected traditional Christianity"[83] and "Part of Dickinson's preoccupation with death stems doubtlessly from her rejection of Christ. . . . she apparently refused to place her faith in Christ, even though she knew the way of salvation. . . . At times she seems orthodox; at other times she is blasphemous."[84]

Henry James, we are told, "professed no religious beliefs at all and substituted the worship of beauty and art for the worship of God."[85] His works "thus give little insight into the spiritual realities of life."[86]

The beloved Mark Twain (Samuel Clemens) "deliberately rejected God"[87] and his writings "reveal the sad history of man's stubborn rebellion against God."[88] Twain's hero Huckleberry Finn "mocks prayer, sees all religious people as naive or hypocritical and rejects traditional standards of right and wrong."[89] Finally, Twain "embodied in his works an increasingly pessimistic view of God and His Word."[90]   The teacher is also admonished, "As you discuss Clemens's biography with the students, point out to them the relationship between his rejection of God and his pessimism."[91]

In the section on the naturalists, the text says that students should be able to "See the pessimism men often fall into when they deny the truth of God's Word."[92] Stephen Crane "represents the broad religious and literary rebellion characteristic of modern literature,"[93] largely because he rejected his parents' devout Methodism. Crane's poetry reveals the author's "quarrel with God."[94]   His poetry "shows in particular the pessimism man sinks into when he denies the Biblical view of God."[95]   In summary, "Crane's work shows as a whole a deliberate rejection of orthodox religious views."[96] The teacher is urged to emphasize that "Crane's life reveals the fate of someone who deliberately rejects God. In Crane's case he had full knowledge of the Biblical description of God, yet his poetry reveals a total and deliberate rejection of that knowledge. The sadness of his life also powerfully illustrates the consequences of such rejection."[97]   A lighthearted attitude toward doom in Crane's poem "Should the Wide World Roll Away" is an occasion for the teacher to warn of "the tragedy that befalls those who reject God. . . ."[98] Hell will be much worse than people can even imagine."[99]

Jack London is not seen as an appealing adventure writer because "he illustrated many of the beliefs central to the socialistic and evolutionary doctrines he had accepted from his wide reading."[100] He "laced his writings with ideas that reveal his enthusiasm for socialist and Darwinian thought."[101] He is also a moral nihilist. "According to London, morality has no place in the real world."[102] Once again, the author of this text uses tragedies in a writer's life to show that people who reject God end up disillusioned and battered. "London's debts piled up, the crops on his farm were ruined, his drinking increased, his health failed, and his second marriage went sour. he even became disillusioned with the socialistic ideas he had earlier embraced.   In 1916—alcoholic, in debt, and weary of life itself—the forty-year-old author died, quite possibly by suicide."[103]   Apparently, nothing bad in this world ever happens to pious Christians, or so the text implies repeatedly.   One can only wonder if students can relate to such a view of life, which seems to many to be profoundly "unbiblical," to use a favorite catchphrase of the Bob Jones University series.   Finally, London's short story "The Law of Life" is to be used by the teacher to "Contrast the Eskimos' (and London's) view of death with the Biblical view."[104]

Frank Norris is dismissed as a writer worthy of respect or emulation for a typical reason: "Apparently Norris never knew the liberating power of the truth of God's Word."[105] Edwin Markham's optimism "lies in his humanistic values."[106] Neither the naturalist poets nor the optimists are acceptable to Christian readers.   "Notice that where the naturalists err in saying there is no God, Markham errs in saying man needs no God."[107]

William Sidney Porter (O. Henry)'s stories are "amusing,"[108] but, "Unfortunately they do not give insight into human life as it is described in God's Word."[109]   The text does include O. Henry's wonderful Christmas tale about unselfishness, "The Gift of the Magi."

The text devotes seven pages to the poems and hymns of the blind author Fanny Crosby.   The text says, "Her poems of joy and faith offer the strongest of all refutations to the bleak pessimism of the American naturalists."[110]   Students be able to "recognize that even in the midst of a generally unbelieving and confused generation, God raises up a testimony to the truth."[111] It is admitted that her poems "sometimes lack high literary quality"[112] but "they express sincere faith coupled with eternal truth"[113] and "are based on Scriptural truths."[114]   Even Crosby, however, was "apparently not saved until she was about thirty years old."[115]

American literature since 1920 is seen as bleak, incoherent, and pessimistic.   Students are warned that "pernicious philosophies confront them at every turn."[116] Modern human beings and modern thought are seen as sinful in every way. "Having abandoned belief in the Bible, modern man has often yielded to pessimism or embraced irrational hope. . . . Many Americans who do not know Christ have lost their traditional optimism and idealism, turned pessimistic, and given themselves over to despair. . . . At the root of modern American thought is the un-Biblical view of man's nature and calling."[117]

In sum, "The spirit of the age—especially disbelief in God, cynical pessimism, and the resulting despair—dominates modern literature."[118]

H. L. Mencken "fiercely attacked anyone who advocated traditional moral restraints"[119] and "openly repudiated the nation's inherited system of values and beliefs."[120] Writers who resided in Greenwich Village "displayed the intensity of their hatred for traditional morality by experimenting with various forms of moral license."[121] John Steinbeck's *Grapes of Wrath* "spreads its own brand of humanistic religion"[122] through the character of Jim Casy, who "utters Steinbeck's moral view."[123] Edwin Arlington Robinson "concentrated on the negative side of human existence."[124] "Robinson's rejection of Christ is the root cause of his pessimism and lack of any substantial hope."[125]

Even religious novels "have absorbed the spirit of the age."[126] Lloyd Douglas's *The Robe* "portrays several key liberal notions."[127] The text despises Sinclair Lewis's *Elmer Gantry*, a satire on the hypocrisy and excesses of revivalism in the 1920s. This text engages in grotesque distortions by claiming that "Lewis portrays atheistic churchmen on all ecclesiastical levels serving only themselves and their earthly ambitions."[128] The text claims that Lewis got his ideas for the novel from "a Roman Catholic priest, a rabbi, and the city's chief agnostic."[129] Lewis "also provided liquor to loosen their tongues."[130] This is the author's idea of a serious explanation of the genesis of a major American novel.

Robert Frost may be a beloved poet who enriched American literature and who graced a Presidential inauguration, but this text portrays him as "bitter in his rejection of Biblical truth"[131] and as one who "leaves virtually no place for God."[132] The text explains further: "Although attracted at times to Biblical themes and stories, Frost remained modern in the subjectivity of his belief and his religious doubt. . . . He tried, as it were, to walk a middle course between faith and denial. His keeping to a middle way would perhaps seem reasonable if there were no right way. But since God reveals a right way to mankind, Frost's middle way misses the mark. . . ."[133] Therefore, "Frost's poetry proposes a humanistic answer to man's problems."[134]

Carl Sandburg may have been a notable and popular celebrant of the American experience, but this text says, "His moral values and view of man, unfortunately, are not those of the Word of God. In fact, Sandburg's work consistently shows sympathy with forces denying Biblical truth."[135] In addition, we are told, "Sandburg's works often lack careful craftmanship. One reason is that they generally served as vehicles for his socialistic views. The concern of the propagandist overshadowed the concern of the artist. Sandburg's propagandism certainly does not recommend him to Christians or to conservatives generally. In one poem he attacked the evangelist Billy Sunday; in another he defended the anarchists Sacco and Vanzetti."[136]

E. E. Cummings's "view of life is incompatible with a Christian philosophy"[137] and Wallace Stevens "rejects outright the Word of God. . ."[138] About Stevens's poem "Sunday Morning" we are informed: "Its rejection of Christ's incarnation and the soul's immortality is typical of modern religious unbelief. It sets aside Biblical answers to age-old questions about death and life after death, substituting a neo-pagan religious view of the world[139]. . . The poet substitutes the worship of nature for the worship of God.[140] . . . In this poem Stevens thus embodies the view of the modern man who has renounced the truth of God's Word."[141]

James Weldon Johnson's "The Creation," which celebrates black preachers and their oratorical style, is not favorably
depicted. "Although *God's Trombones* uses Biblical material,
the poet's real interest is the black heritage of religious expression, not the Biblical material itself. In fact, Johnson regarded
his material as mere legend or myth, a view with which modern
liberalism is altogether sympathetic."[142]   Shirley Jackson's
"attraction to demonology and abnormality" in her stories "mars
them for Christian readers."[143]   One of her characters "violates
Biblical principles" because of his "open defiance of authority."[144]

Ernest Hemingway's "notorious definition of morality .
. . totally ignores God's moral laws."[145]   "It is no wonder then
that those who hold this view of life can only, like Hemingway,
come to despair."[146]   Hemingway's suicide is pointedly noted.

There is hardly a praiseworthy item in the anthology.
One exception is T. S. Eliot and his exceptional poem "Journey
of the Magi."   The author praises Eliot as "The only major
literary voice to speak in support of Christianity,"[147] though
Eliot's Anglo-Catholicism is not a respected option to the Bob
Jones University series of texts.   Archibald Rutledge is praised
for his "traditional moral perspective"[148] and Thornton
Wilder's "works include values such as honesty, love and faith
in the providence of God which the Christian reader can
appreciate."[149]   The local colorists and regionalists like Bret
Harte, Sidney Lanier, Hamlin Garland, and Jesse Stuart are at
least treated in a neutral manner.   James Whitcomb Riley's
poems are admired because they celebrate optimism and rural
life, where simplicity and virtue allegedly remain.

One additional failure of this text is its inability to
understand that when fiction becomes religious propaganda, it
ceases to be good fiction.   Fiction, even religious fiction, should
suggest religious values in implicit terms and with artistry and
imagination.   Heavy-handed didactic fiction fails as genuine
literature.   Is it any wonder that few, if any, major writers come
from fundamentalist or evangelical Protestant backgrounds and

that fewer still practice this religion, whose ethos is so hostile to values generally cherished by the literary community. The contrast with the large number of writers who are or have been Catholic, Jewish, Anglican or religiously liberal is instructive. Some religions seem to enhance the literary imagination while others repress it.

This attack on writers and the literary life is puzzling in a book that is supposed to explore the meaning and matter of literature and presumably to give some appreciation for books and creative literature. If all—or most—of literature is evil and offensive to God and Biblical values, why should students read at all? Will this course encourage them to read widely, to sample the joys of literature?

This text shows no indication of the joys or struggles of the literary life, its hardships and rejections or of the satisfaction it often brings to writers and the pleasure it affords readers. There is no appreciation of the life of the mind, the integrity of the intellectual life, or of the author's intent to maintain high standards of artistic integrity.

Pensacola Christian College's "A Beka Book" series devoted to America"s literary heritage resonates with similar religious biases.

Most of the selections in one guide to early American literature are religious in nature and inspiration. At least half of the material reflects spiritual concerns and a preoccupation with death. Included are sermons and essays by Increase Mather, Jonathan Edwards' "Sinners in the Hands of An Angry God," Michael Wigglesworth's "Day of Doom," and "The Bay Psalm Book." Students read many excellent religious poems and Negro spirituals. They also read sermons by DeWitt Talmage and Billy Sunday, a self-educated ex-baseball player whose "writings" would seem more appropriate to a speech course than to one on literature. About Sunday we read, "His clear, colorful down-to-earth sermons helped keep America from being destroyed by religious liberalism and moral degradation at the beginning of the twentieth century."[150]

Writers are frequently depicted as unhappy and unbalanced. About Edgar Allan Poe we read, "It is always a pity that Poe, apparently always unstable, turned to drink, deteriorating physically and emotionally until his death at the age of forty."[151]   Ambrose Bierce "detested his pious father and was ashamed of his whole family because they were religious.[152] . . . He had an unhappy personal life: he separated from his wife, lost his two sons, and broke many friendships. After he went to Mexico in 1913, he was never seen again."[153]   Stephen Crane, "whose father was a Methodist minister and writer of tracts, and whose mother was a writer and editor of Christian publications, rebelled against his Christian heritage. . . . Crane did not recognize sin as sin but attempted to blame man's behavior on social, economic, and environmental forces."[154]   Mark Twain "became very depressed in his later years and developed a pessimistic view of human nature."[155]

Some attempts are made to emphasize the religious character of certain literary figures. Benjamin Franklin's appeal for prayer and remembrance of God at the Constitutional Convention is mentioned.[156]   Dictionary compiler and textbook author Noah Webster is represented in part by an essay extolling the exclusive virtues of Christianity. "Let your first care through life, be directed to support and extend the influence of the Christian religion, and the observance of the sabbath. This is the only system of religion which has ever been offered to the consideration and acceptance of men, which has even probable evidence of a divine origin; it is the only religion that honors the character and moral government of the Supreme Being; it is the only religion which gives even a probable account of the origin of the world, and of the dispensations of God towards mankind; it is the only religion which teaches the character and laws of God, with our relations and our duties to him; it is the only religion which assures of us of an immortal existence; which offers the means of everlasting salvation, and consoles mankind under the inevitable calamities of the present life."[157]

Anne Bradstreet's poems are commended because "all of her works have as their ultimate purpose the glorification of God."[158] Michael Wigglesworth's "Day of Doom" is admired because it is "a striking picture of the Judgment Day as God listens to and answers those sinners pleading for mercy."[159]

The main selection is Nathaniel Hawthorne's novel *The Scarlet Letter*, chosen apparently because it is a trenchant study of sin and guilt and because Hawthorne opposed "ungodly free thinkers"[160] and "was convinced of man's innate sinful nature."[161] In this novel, we are told, "Every character is a study in fallen human nature and presents a different reaction to sin."[162]

About Hester Prynne's sin we are told, "Hawthorne, however, never tells us if she ever asked God's forgiveness for her sin . . . Hester never seemed to realize that to be saved, she must recognize her sin, realize that she cannot help herself, and accept Christ who died for sinners to pardon and save her."[163] Furthermore, "Wearing the scarlet letter cannot take the place of individual, personal repentance which is the first step in having sins forgiven."[164]

The text criticizes Hawthorne's satire on Puritan gloom. "Hawthorne's is an exaggerated view of Puritan seriousness. The Biblical view of joy and happiness is that man can only find true joy when he can fellowship with God and enjoy communion with Him."[165]

Students are warned that they must be careful what they read in all instances. "A reader must be careful not to allow the ideas presented in a literary work to determine his beliefs or be the basis of his perception of truth; all ideas should be tested in the light of God's Word."[166]

The fourth volume in the *Classics for Christians* series looks at American writers and "evaluates them in the light of the truths of God's Word."[167] The selections reveal some religious bias, though it is much less apparent than in the Bob Jones University series.

The longest selection in this text is from Lew Wallace's *Ben Hur*, "a tale of the Christ" written while the author was undergoing conversion to Christianity. Also included are hymns by Fanny Crosby, sermon selections from Dwight Moody, T. DeWitt Talmage, and Billy Sunday, and a religious meditation from A. W. Tozer. There is, in addition, "Ten Reasons Why I Believe the Bible is the Word of God," by R. A. Torry, who is called "a great soulwinner to skeptics, infidels, and atheists."[168]   None of these writers would be considered top-flight or representative of the best of American literature.   The biography section also includes material from Elisabeth Elliot, a missionary whose husband was slain by head-hunters in Ecuador. And, there is "A Father's Prayer" by Douglas MacArthur.

The discussion of most authors is negative. Writers seem to have a penchant for rejecting religious truth and moral values. "Many writers . . . did not want to be hemmed in by the traditional (Biblical) morality that prevailed across much of the land.   To get away from the influence of Biblical Christianity, many writers and others who thought of themselves as intellectuals moved to Europe. . ."[169]

H. L. Mencken, one of America's finest writers and literary geniuses, is reviled. "H. L. Mencken, an outspoken literary critic who was hostile to Christianity, led the way for other critics to make fun of anything that was wholesome, conservative, or sacred."[170]

Modern literature is much too influenced by European infidelity.   "European natural scientists, theologians, and philosophers had been at work undermining the Scriptural beliefs and values that built Western civilization."[171]

Naturalism in literature "is an attempt to understand man and nature apart from the Scriptures . . . Since the natural man must inevitably end in failure, Naturalistic literature is always pessimistic, demoralizing, or sad."[172] Sigmund Freud "tries to excuse man's sin."[173]

A strong bias against the writing profession pervades the text.   "It is no wonder that . . . so much recent American literature is negative and pessimistic. Nor are we surprised to find that the lives of so many artists ended in hopelessness and despair."[174]   This is reiterated in biographical discussions of prominent writers. Thus, about Edgar Allan Poe, we read, "His pride, temper, and emotional outbreaks caused conflicts wherever he went. After his wife's death, he continually battled against illness, emotional problems, and poverty. He turned to drink and deteriorated physically and emotionally until his death at the age of forty."[175]   On William Faulkner: "Most of the qualities Faulkner admired are Christian virtues, but because he divorced them from their source, he was never able to truly attain them in his writings or his life. Faulkner, like Hemingway, drank heavily at times and used alcohol as an escape from his pressures."[176]   Vachel Lindsay's "life proves that a life of art alone is not sufficient for happiness. As his poetic powers failed, he became disillusioned and committed suicide."[177]

Sara Teasdale "lived a solitary life and was often ill. She suffered a nervous breakdown and was disturbed when she heard of Vachel Lindsay's suicide. About a year after Lindsay's death, she also committed suicide."[178]   F. Scott Fitzgerald "eventually had a mental breakdown . . . and died an alcoholic at the age of forty-four."[179]   (Actually, he died of a heart attack.) Ernest Hemingway "married four times, drank heavily, was hospitalized for mental depression, and finally took his own life."[180]   This dreary repetition of the travails of the writing life can hardly commend the profession to students, especially when it is not balanced by depictions of the happy and successful lives of some other major authors.

Some classics are interpreted from the perspective of religious bias. Archibald MacLeish's retelling of the story of Job is labeled "un-Scriptural,[181] while Sinclair Lewis's *Elmer Gantry* presents "an unrealistic view of Christianity and religion in general."[182]   Many critics regard *J. B.* as a sensitive and refreshing look at the Book of Job and *Elmer Gantry* as a realistic, true-to-life portrait of the excesses of revivalism. Herman Melville's *Moby Dick* shows "the awful *consequences of deliberately choosing evil over good.* It deals with the attempt of a man to become a god by violating universal laws established by God."[183]

The text is sharply critical of Ralph Waldo Emerson and the Transcendentalist movement. "New England, which was conceived and nurtured by the Puritans and other dedicated Christians of the seventeenth century, almost had its foundations torn away in the nineteenth century by the false religion of Unitarianism and its religio-philosophical counterpart, Transcendentalism."[184] Transcendentalism was really "the old pantheistic nature worship of the pagans blended with a heightened worship of man."[185] And, "The basic mistake of Transcendentalism was self-trust, and the essence of the movement was selfishness. . ."[186] Transcendentalism has led to even greater evils. "Preposterous as it is, the idea, which is as old as man's first rebellion against God, keeps coming back in dimly masqueraded forms. In our day, it can be seen as Modernism (religious Liberalism), Secular Humanism, civil disobedience, the worship of nature, transcendental meditation, and all forms of disrespect for authority and rebellion against Scriptural principles."[187]

Emerson's poetry, we are informed, "shows his deep ignorance of the Scriptures" and rejects the Bible and the divinity of Christ.[188]   In a later discussion we are told, "Emerson admired the fruits of Christianity even though he tried to cut himself off from its roots. Because of this, he had many of the outward virtues of the Christian life, including kindness, morality, sincerity, and optimism. His blindness to important spiritual truths led him and his followers to personal disaster, however, and opened the way to a multitude of false teachings."[189]   But, "His attempts at arriving at spiritual truth through his own understanding, however, should always be spurned."[190]

Emerson's contemporary, Henry David Thoreau, "despised governments and lived in contempt of man and society,"[191] and "failed to recognize that government was ordained by God."[192] Thoreau's views particularly corrupted people who lived in the 1960s. "The political views which he expressed in 'Civil Disobedience' became popular a hundred years after his death, and they have led to much disorder, violence, and anarchy in the name of peace, rights, and individualism."[193]

There are selections from J. Gresham Machen and Alexander Solzhenitsyn's 1978 Harvard University commencement address on "the threat of humanism."[194] Also admired is A. W. Tozer, whose "acceptance of the Bible as the supreme authority gave him a firm foundation for understanding the writings of men . . ."[195] A selection of "Wisdom for the Twentieth Century" includes pious proclamations on the importance of the Bible by Presidents Herbert Hoover, Theodore Roosevelt, and Woodrow Wilson.[196]

Detailed discussions of British literature are largely devoted to attacks on Catholicism and Anglicanism, and thus have been discussed elsewhere. The volumes also show distinct preferences for those few writers who exemplify evangelical Protestant value systems. Literary history is interpreted in the same light as political and religious history.

One literature text devotes attention to religious issues apparent in the Elizabethan period.

Samuel Rutherford was a "strict Presbyterian" while Richard Baxter was a "moderate Anglican."[197] Baxter is admired by the author since Baxter "was appalled by the profane lives of the clergy" and later became a preacher whose "converts multiplied and swelled the congregation."[198] Because of Baxter's devotional books, "saints grew rich in knowledge and faith."[199] Both Rutherford and Baxter, we are informed, "understood that the only true basis of Christian unity is belief in the fundamental doctrines of God's Word."[200] The text also claims that both writers are safely in heaven, "having been home together three hundred years in 'the saints' everlasting rest.'"[201]

This text adores John Milton, who receives 24 pages of text, and John Bunyan, who gets 21 pages. However, even

Milton strayed from the narrow path of fundamentalist salvation by being too liberal on subjects like divorce and censorship. These views, however, "arose from his personal circumstances and not from an objective study of Scripture."[202] Milton may even have veered dangerously close to Unitarianism. "Late in life he apparently adopted an Arian concept of the Trinity—the heretical view that the Son is not co-equal with the Father."[203] Nevertheless, his *Paradise Lost* "may be appreciated as a great Christian poem"[204] because "it shows the Son of God in His scriptural roles as Creator and Redeemer"[205] and "represents man's good in terms of submission to divine authority. . ."[206]

John Bunyan is seen as a true hero who "came under strong conviction of sin and fear of damnation, repented, and found assurance of salvation."[207] His allegory *Pilgrim's Progress* is hailed as a "literary masterpiece" because "Bunyan's work differs from its modern successors in offering a purposeful view of life and a reassuring conclusion—those of the Christian life."[208]

The second volume by the same author is replete with examples of judgmentalism, the quasi-infallible ability of Bob Jones University textbook authors to know the sincerity and integrity of the religious convictions of the authors included. We are constantly being informed about the religious beliefs and values of the writers. We are told that William Butler Yeats was "an unbeliever in Christianity,"[209] that D. H. Lawrence's writings are filled with "shocking blasphemy and immorality,"[210] but that an obscure author, Benjamin Robert Haydon, had a "deep respect for Christian truth."[211]

Two baffling passages make literary claims for Protestantism which many scholars would question. "Rustic eloquence is not found in regions untouched by the Protestant Reformation. . . . The key to understanding Shakespeare is not German transcendentalism or modern existentialism but the truths of the Protestant Reformation."[212] If anything, Shakespeare's religious imagery is substantially Catholic.[213]

Robert Burns receives ambivalent treatment. Criticized because "his drinking songs and romantic ballads flaunted the sins that were increasingly scandalizing the town,"[214] Burns "resented restraint of any kind and held, with the rationalists, to the natural goodness of man."[215] But he is praised for writing "The Cotter's Saturday Night" (a selection chosen for the text) because it portrays favorably the Bible-loving peasants of Scotland.

Conservative political writers are clearly preferred. Edmund Burke's view of man "is essentially Christian,"[216] while Thomas Paine is called "a revolutionary propagandist,"[217] and "a radical deist"[218] whose *Age of Reason* is "a coarse attack on Christianity."[219]

William Wordsworth's poetry is seen this way: "As the vehicle of a surrogate religion, it trumpets the spiritual apostasy of Western man."[220]

The portrait of Thomas Carlyle is full of dire warnings for Christian youth. "The history of Carlyle's youth is the sad story, often repeated, of the gifted young man with high purpose and principles sent by well-intentioned, godly parents to a center of secular learning to prepare for the service of God. Having entered Edinburgh University at the age of fifteen, the ambitious, sensitive youth encountered ideas in his reading that undermined his Presbyterian faith. Confused and embittered, he left the university without taking a degree. . ."[221] Carlyle became a disillusioned rationalist whose "message was another gospel, a false hope."[222] There is little good in Carlyle. "What today remains instructive and inspirational in Carlyle are these great truths he retained from his Presbyterian upbringing . . .[223]

Thomas Hardy's "pessimistic fiction and poetry show as well as any writing of the period the eroding effect of Victorian rationalism on religious faith."[224]

Victorian literature is called a "blend of moralism and melancholy"[225] largely because "England by 1897 had forgotten the spiritual source of her material greatness and was already in decline."[226] Nostalgia for the hightide of evangelicalism is seen in these passages. "Church attendance throughout England was expected and remained high. Sunday sports were discouraged, and family Bible reading was prevalent. John Wesley had preached public morality as well as spiritual conversion. . . . missionaries streamed from England to every corner of the Empire, and Britain undertook to evangelize as well as civilize the pagan nations of the world. It is clear that Victorian economic success and colonial expansion had a moral foundation and that this foundation rested in turn on vital Christian faith."[227]

Tragically, all of this was coming to an end. "By the end of the century both this faith and the morality it supported were disintegrating, and England was losing the blessing of God. The sons of prosperous middle-class merchants had lost their evangelical beliefs at the preparatory schools and the universities. Some had turned to agnosticism; some, to such religious substitutes as transcendentalism, traditionalism (Roman or High Anglican), and aestheticism (the worship of beauty). Biblical historicity had been challenged by German biblical scholarship and Darwinian evolutionary theory. The lengthening shadows of religious doubt cast a gloom over the closing decades of Victoria's reign, and Britain faced the trials of the new century without the spiritual assurance that had buoyed her in the past."[228] Students are warned, "The informed Christian will not fail to see the lesson of England's fortunes since 1688. Despite spiritual and material benefits almost unparalleled in the history of European nations since the Middle Ages, England declared her moral and intellectual independence from the Author of those benefits. . . . enslavement follows the attempt to be free from accountability to God."[229]

William Blake's poetry is dismissed in this fashion. "What we have in Blake is obviously a Satanic counterfeit of Christian redemption, a visionary outlook that has increasingly prevailed in our own time. The modern drive toward unity—political, social, racial, and religious—urged on by a deep sense of alienation stems from the thinking of Blake and his contemporaries. Cultural togetherness, as a goal, is central to secular humanism, the modern religion of man."[230]

This book's selectivity reinforces its sectarian tone. In addition to the standard writers, passages from Isaac Watts' hymns, John Wesley's sermons, Charles Wesley's hymns and Charles Spurgeon's sermons are treated as important examples of modern English literature.

In the Pensacola series authors Anderson and Hicks argue that *all* classics must be "true, honest, just, pure, lovely and of good report," echoing St. Paul's Epistle to the Philippians. The authors argue that "people who do wrong must be shown to ultimately fail or repent of their wrong. People who do right must be shown to ultimately triumph. Goodness must be praised and evil condemned."[231] Classics must also make readers feel pure and elevated. ". . .the books that have lasted put a premium on purity."[232]

The religious content in selectivity is very high. Students read selections from seven hymn writers of the eighteenth century, and four devotional books by Matthew Henry, William Law, George Whitefield and John Wesley. Most of William Cowper's poems included in the text are devotional in nature since "the solace that his troubled mind found in Christ has given us some of our most comforting hymns."[233] Four hymn writers of the romantic age are included. They are followed by twelve "Victorian preachers and hymn writers," including Charles Haddon Spurgeon, Frances Ridley Havergal and Horatius Bonar. The Victorian poetry section includes frankly religious poems by Christina Rossetti, Gerard Manley Hopkins, Coventry Patmore, George MacDonald and Francis Thompson.

The twentieth century is represented by "devotional works" from Campbell Morgan, John Jowett, Oswald Chambers and Amy Carmichael. There are selections from C. S. Lewis and Malcom Muggeridge. In "The Romantic Age" section, poems are selected which symbolize the battle between "pantheism and a personal God."

Nearly one fourth of the literary selections (102 pages out of 444) are directly religious, addressing spiritual themes in poetry, hymnody, essay, and short fiction. Some are high quality, e.g., T. S. Eliot's "Journey of the Magi," C. S. Lewis's *Screwtape Letters*, Tennyson's "St. Agnes Eve" and "Crossing the Bar" and Rudyard Kipling's "Recessional," while others are of questionable literary value.

The authors clearly believe that "the literature of Great Britain is a reflection of the spiritual state of the British people through the ages. Perhaps no other body of literature in the world so eloquently portrays the truth of Proverbs 14:34: 'Righteousness exalteth a nation: but sin is a reproach to any people.' The history of English literature began with the introduction of Christianity to the land. Literature reached a low point during the spiritual darkness of the Middle Ages and rose to unprecedented heights of excellence with the return of the Bible in the days of Elizabeth I and of the Puritans."[234] This theme is reiterated. The Restoration era was "licentious," the eighteenth century was dominated by the "barrenness of deism," the Victorian era was "creative" and the twentieth century is a period of "decline in faith, morality, thought and letters."[235] Still, "even in the worst of times, God has raised up exceptional men and women who, with their eyes fixed on Him, have risen above their times to produce great classics."[236]

The late seventeenth century was dominated by "cold intellect" and a lack of morals.[237] "False philosophy led to loose morals"[238] because "the philosophy of the period left out the Bible."[239]

Alexander Pope's "Essay on Man" comes in for strong criticism because it allegedly "treats God only as an impersonal Creator and emphasizes man's reason over God's revealed Word. Pope recognizes God's order and design in the universe, but he believes that man's knowledge cannot extend beyond the limits of his own reason. . . . Pope fails to recognize God's Word as the final source of understanding."[240]

William Blackstone is admired because he is supposed to have believed that "'Natural Law' must be determined by obedience to Revealed Law, the Word of God."[241]   Samuel Johnson is praised because "He was a staunch supporter of the Bible against the claims of deism. He went against the tide of his day in his stand for the Bible."[242]

Religion is a major factor in how this text interprets the lives and literary value of many writers. Robert Burns's poems "reflect the high standards of the Bible-loving Scots."[243] George Bernard Shaw "denied Christianity," "ridiculed the Christian morals of his time," was "arrogant in his writings" and "advocated salvation through political reform."[244]   One reason that Shaw was so confused is that he "allowed Henrik Ibsen to formulate his thinking," even though Ibsen "destroyed the morals of the people" in his plays.[245]

William Wordsworth "was too optimistic in his view of nature and man's human nature to recognize that both are fallen. He tended toward pantheism, the false idea that the spirit of God dwells in nature and that to commune with nature is to commune with God."[246]   Matthew Arnold is criticized because "He believes he can achieve happiness through self-realization, an idea that goes contrary to the Scriptural principle of Matthew 10:39."[247]   However, the text is pleased because Wordsworth and Samuel Taylor Coleridge rejected liberal politics and religion and became "orthodox" Christians in their later years.[248]

This text loathes the great triumvirate of English Romantics, Byron, Shelley and Keats. "Byron's entire life seemed to be unstable and rebellious. . . . he lived a dissolute life of self-indulgence and became involved in scandalous love affairs."[249] It wasn't all Byron's fault, however, since "women threw themselves at him."[250] ". . . Percy Bysshe Shelley "lived a life of rebellion against God, morality, society, and government."[251]

Shelley's writings on atheism are "crude and foolish," and he wasted his life on "radical politics, and in stirring up the people of Ireland to rebel against England."[252]   John Keats had "a life filled with sorrow,"[253] because he "refused the Bible, the only book that could show him how to have his name written in the Lamb's book of Life. . ."[254]

England, under Queen Victoria's moral leadership, is lionized as "a nation exalted by righteousness."[255] "Britain reaped a double blessing during most of Victoria's reign—the blessing of having a righteous ruler (Proverbs 29:2) and the blessing that is promised to a nation whose people live by principles of righteousness (Proverbs 14:34)."[256] Thus, "Victorians aspired to live moral lives in line with their understanding of the Scriptures, and their high standards enabled them to excel in literature, science, and industry in a way that is still admired today."[257]

Protestantism was responsible for this moral grandeur. "The Bible gave England the Protestant work ethic, the Biblical teaching that God expects all men to work and that work is a noble duty to be performed toward God."[258] Also, "The Bible gave the Victorians a compassion for others that is almost unparalleled in history."[259] It was not Anglicans, Roman Catholics, Jews, or liberal Protestants who deserve this praise. "The Evangelicals and Dissenters were often scorned by other churchmen, but history has shown that they were the ones who had the greatest impact for good on British society."[260] These evangelicals "stressed personal salvation and Christian living,"[261] which other Christians apparently ignored.

Victorian education is also seen as a model. "In Victorian England, education had been viewed as a way to train each individual to use his God-given abilities for the glory of God and the edification of his fellow man."[262]

Needless to say, very few historians agree with this roseate interpretation of Victorian England.

The "three great poets" of the Victorian era are evaluated in the light of the text's religious bias. Lord Tennyson "developed a strong faith in God"[263] and Robert Browning "wrote optimistic and encouraging poems also based on an underlying Christian philosophy. Matthew Arnold, however, could never accept Christian faith as the answer to the problems of his day, and as a result his poems are not as hopeful."[264]

Other late nineteenth century writers are criticized for their religious and moral failures. The "immoral" Oscar Wilde "died a broken, disillusioned, lonely man."[265] William Ernest Henley's poem "Invictus" "is a poor substitute for the strength and peace a Christian finds in Christ . . . Instead of finding comfort and peace in God, Henley seems to think that he alone must master his fate."[266] Thomas Hardy wrote "brooding, pessimistic" novels[267] because "he did not believe in God."[268] Hardy's poem "The Respectable Burgher" gives this text a chance to condemn "the 'scholarly' but ungodly men in Germany" who dared to apply the principles of higher criticism to the Bible. Because of them, "many clergy and their people fell under the influence of this liberal thought, and the Bible, the church, and Christianity in general lost credibility."[269]

Twentieth century writers are pathetic because "some of the most talented used their God-given abilities to tear down the Christian values that had made England great. . . . Many writers hastened England's decay by using their talents to attack Christianity and promote materialism through the redistribution of wealth."[270] Sweeping generalizations abound in this section of the text. It is claimed that "fiction in the twentieth century has been marked by an ignorance of Christianity and a disillusionment with society."[271] About H. G. Wells we are told, "In his last book he very wisely repudiated everything he had ever said or written."[272]

W. H. Auden "embraced Christianity, though he continued to follow Freudian teachings,"[273] which may be a veiled reference to Auden's homosexuality. Dylan Thomas "was almost as renowned for his infamous life style as for his works. He had a very stormy marriage with his wife Caitlin and drank heavily. . . . he died in New York of pneumonia contracted from his acute alcoholism."[274] James Joyce "rejected all values" of his upbringing, "ran away with an uneducated chambermaid," had two children with her but "never actually married" until years later and then only at "the insistence of their mentally ill daughter."[275] This text seems to delight in poking fun at writers and suggesting that independent-minded free spirits are doomed to live unsatisfactory lives.

A guide to England's literary life from the early Middle Ages to the Puritans[276] is characterized by a strong religious orientation. Almost half of the book (163 out of 339 pages of text) is devoted to religious writings. The longest selection is a 78-page excerpt from John Bunyan's *Pilgrim's Progress*. There are also long selections from *Paradise Lost* and from various religious and metaphysical poets.

A marked preference is shown toward the Puritan writers. More material is devoted to them than to all of medieval and early Elizabethan literature. Included is a four-page section of quotations called "The Wisdom of the Puritans," extolling strict Christian behavior and the inerrancy of the Scriptures.

NOTES

1. Raymond A. St. John, *American Literature for Christian Schools, Book 2, (Realism, Naturalism, and Modern American Literature)*, Teacher's Edition (Greenville, SC: Bob Jones University Press, 1991), p. 544.

2. *Ibid.*, p. 544.

3. *Ibid.*, p. 544.

4. *Ibid.*, p. 544.

5. *Ibid.*, p. 544.

6. *Ibid.*, p. 546.

7. *Ibid.*, p. 546.

8. *Ibid.*, p. 546.

9. *Ibid.*, p. 546.

10. *Ibid.*, p. 546.

11. Glen Chambers and Gene Fisher, *United States History for Christian Schools* (Greenville, SC: Bob Jones University Press, 1982), p. 459.

12. Raymond A. St. John, *American Literature for Christian Schools, Book 1, (Early American Literature and American*

Romanticism), Teacher's Edition (Greenville, SC: Bob Jones University Press, 1991), p. 2.

13. *Ibid.*, p. 4.
14. *Ibid.*, p. 6.
15. *Ibid.*, p. 13.
16. *Ibid.*, p. 12.
17. *Ibid.*, p. 80.
18. *Ibid.*, p. 79.
19. *Ibid.*, p. 29.
20. *Ibid.*, p. 23.
21. *Ibid.*, p. 95.
22. *Ibid.*, p. 95.
23. *Ibid.*, p. 95.
24. *Ibid.*, p. 95.
25. *Ibid.*, p. 110.
26. *Ibid.*, p. 111.
27. *Ibid.*, p. 111.
28. *Ibid.*, p. 114.
29. *Ibid.*, p. 117.
30. *Ibid.*, p. 117.
31. *Ibid.*, p. 117.
32. *Ibid.*, p. 117.
33. *Ibid.*, p. 117.
34. *Ibid.*, p. 120.
35. *Ibid.*, p. 120.
36. *Ibid.*, p. 127.
37. *Ibid.*, p. 126.
38. *Ibid.*, p. 128.
39. *Ibid.*, p. 145.
40. *Ibid.*, p. 140.
41. *Ibid.*, p. 171.
42. *Ibid.*, p. 171.
43. *Ibid.*, p. 173.
44. *Ibid.*, p. 149.
45. *Ibid.*, p. 183.
46. *Ibid.*, p. 190.

47. *Ibid.*, p. 193.
48. *Ibid.*, p. 179.
49. *Ibid.*, p. 163.
50. *Ibid.*, p. 164.
51. *Ibid.*, p. 196.
52. *Ibid.*, p. 197.
53. *Ibid.*, p. 198.
54. *Ibid.*, p. 202.
55. *Ibid.*, p. 202.
56. *Ibid.*, p. 209.
57. *Ibid.*, p. 214.
58. *Ibid.*, p. 214.
59. *Ibid.*, p. 215.
60. *Ibid.*, p. 223.
61. *Ibid.*, p. 225.
62. *Ibid.*, p. 223.
63. *Ibid.*, p. 222.
64. *Ibid.*, p. 228.
65. *Ibid.*, p. 224.
66. *Ibid.*, p. 243.
67. *Ibid.*, pp. 241-242.
68. *Ibid.*, p. 242.
69. *Ibid.*, p. 263.
70. *Ibid.*, p. 263.
71. *Ibid.*, p. 265.
72. *Ibid.*, p. 307.
73. *Ibid.*, p. 308.
74. *Ibid.*, p. 308.
75. St. John, *American Literature for Christian Schools, Book 2*, p. 346.
76. *Ibid.*, p. 345.
77. *Ibid.*, p. 345.
78. *Ibid.*, p. 364.
79. *Ibid.*, p. 364.
80. *Ibid.*, p. 394.
81. *Ibid.*, p. 405.

82. *Ibid.*, p. 408.
83. *Ibid.*, p. 409.
84. *Ibid.*, p. 414.
85. *Ibid.*, p. 434.
86. *Ibid.*, p. 434.
87. *Ibid.*, p. 454.
88. *Ibid.*, p. 454.
89. *Ibid.*, p. 454.
90. *Ibid.*, p. 453.
91. *Ibid.*, p. 453.
92. *Ibid.*, p. 478.
93. *Ibid.*, p. 478.
94. *Ibid.*, p. 479.
95. *Ibid.*, p. 480.
96. *Ibid.*, p. 480.
97. *Ibid.*, p. 482.
98. *Ibid.*, pp. 482-483.
99. *Ibid.*, pp. 480-481.
100. *Ibid.*, p. 493.
101. *Ibid.*, p. 494.
102. *Ibid.*, p. 494.
103. *Ibid.*, p. 494.
104. *Ibid.*, p. 494.
105. *Ibid.*, p. 502.
106. *Ibid.*, p. 514.
107. *Ibid.*, p. 515.
108. *Ibid.*, p. 581.
109. *Ibid.*, p. 519.
110. *Ibid.*, p. 523.
111. *Ibid.*, p. 523.
112. *Ibid.*, p. 525.
113. *Ibid.*, p. 525.
114. *Ibid.*, p. 525.
115. *Ibid.*, p. 524.
116. *Ibid.*, p. 532.
117. *Ibid.*, p. 536.

118. *Ibid.*, p. 544.
119. *Ibid.*, p. 545.
120. *Ibid.*, p. 545.
121. *Ibid.*, p. 545.
122. *Ibid.*, pp. 546-547.
123. *Ibid.*, p. 547.
124. *Ibid.*, p. 551.
125. *Ibid.*, p. 557.
126. *Ibid.*, p. 543.
127. *Ibid.*, p. 543.
128. *Ibid.*, p. 544.
129. *Ibid.*, p. 544.
130. *Ibid.*, p. 544.
131. *Ibid.*, p. 560.
132. *Ibid.*, p. 561.
133. *Ibid.*, p. 561.
134. *Ibid.*, p. 561.
135. *Ibid.*, p. 589.
136. *Ibid.*, p. 589.
137. *Ibid.*, p. 595.
138. *Ibid.*, p. 600.
139. *Ibid.*, p. 600.
140. *Ibid.*, p. 601.
141. *Ibid.*, p. 605.
142. *Ibid.*, p. 607.
143. *Ibid.*, p. 616.
144. *Ibid.*, p. 621.
145. *Ibid.*, p. 660.
146. *Ibid.*, p. 660.
147. *Ibid.*, p. 611.
148. *Ibid.*, p. 643.
149. *Ibid.*, p. 675.
150. Jan Anderson and Laurel Hicks, *Beginnings of American Literature, Classics for Christians, Vol. 3* (Pensacola, FL: Pensacola Christian College, A Beka Book Publication, 1982), p. 174.

151. *Ibid.*, p. 65.
152. *Ibid.*, p. 85.
153. *Ibid.*, p. 85.
154. *Ibid.*, p. 90.
155. *Ibid.*, p. 39.
156. *Ibid.*, p. 228.
157. *Ibid.*, p. 231.
158. *Ibid.*, p. 241.
159. *Ibid.*, p. 245.
160. *Ibid.*, p. 385.
161. *Ibid.*, p. 272.
162. *Ibid.*, p. 295.
163. *Ibid.*, p. 336, 337.
164. *Ibid.*, p. 345.
165. *Ibid.*, p. 371.
166. *Ibid.*, p. 385.
167. Jan Anderson and Laurel Hicks, *The Literature of the American People, Classics for Christians, Vol. 4* (Pensacola, FL: Pensacola Christian College, A Beka Book Publications, 1983), p. v.
168. *Ibid.*, p. 262.
169. *Ibid.*, p. 252.
170. *Ibid.*, p. 252.
171. *Ibid.*, p. 252.
172. *Ibid.*, p. 253.
173. *Ibid.*, p. 253.
174. *Ibid.*, p. 253.
175. *Ibid.*, p. 8.
176. *Ibid.*, p. 289.
177. *Ibid.*, p. 339.
178. *Ibid.*, p. 342.
179. *Ibid.*, p. 368.
180. *Ibid.*, P. 375.
181. *Ibid.*, p. 350.
182. *Ibid.*, p. 367.
183. *Ibid.*, p. 19.

184. *Ibid.*, p. 91.
185. *Ibid.*, p. 91.
186. *Ibid.*, p. 91.
187. *Ibid.*, p. 92.
188. *Ibid.*, p. 92.
189. *Ibid.*, p. 100.
190. *Ibid.*, p. 100.
191. *Ibid.*, p. 101.
192. *Ibid.*, p. 101.
193. *Ibid.*, p. 101.
194. *Ibid.*, p. 291.
195. *Ibid.*, p. 288.
196. *Ibid.*, p. 293.
197. Ronald A. Horton, *British Literature for Christian Schools: The Early Tradition, 700-1688* (Greenville, SC: Bob Jones University Press, 1982), p. 341.
198. *Ibid.*, p. 342.
199. *Ibid.*, p. 343.
200. *Ibid.*, p. 343.
201. *Ibid.*, p. 343.
202. *Ibid.*, p. 349.
203. *Ibid.*, p. 349.
204. *Ibid.*, p. 350.
205. *Ibid.*, p. 350.
206. *Ibid.*, p. 350.
207. *Ibid.*, p. 375.
208. *Ibid.*, p. 378.
209. Ronald A. Horton, *British Literature for Christian Schools: The Modern Tradition, 1688 to the Present* (Greenville, SC: Bob Jones University Press, 1982), p. 367.
210. *Ibid.*, p. 369.
211. *Ibid.*, p. 254.
212. *Ibid.*, pp. 200-201.
213. For a discussion of Shakespeare's religious imagery see *Shakespeare's Religious Background*, by Peter Milward (Bloomington, IN: Indiana University Press, 1973) and *Shakespeare and*

Catholicism, by Heinrich Mutschmann and Karl Wentersdorf, (New York: Sheed and Ward, 1952).

214. *Ibid.*, p. 152.
215. *Ibid.*, p. 152.
216. *Ibid.*, p. 165.
217. *Ibid.*, p. 166.
218. *Ibid.*, p. 178.
219. *Ibid.*, p. 178.
220. *Ibid.*, p. 189.
221. *Ibid.*, p. 279.
222. *Ibid.*, p. 282.
223. *Ibid.*, p. 282.
224. *Ibid.*, p. 339.
225. *Ibid.*, p. 266.
226. *Ibid.*, p. 260.
227. *Ibid.*, pp. 260-261.
228. *Ibid.*, p. 261.
229. *Ibid.*, p. 258.
230. *Ibid.*, pp. 184-185.
231. Jan Anderson and Laurel Hicks, *The Literature of England, Classics for Christians, Vol. 6* (Pensacola, FL: Pensacola Christian College, A Beka Book Publication, 1983), p. v.
232. *Ibid.*, p. v.
233. *Ibid.*, p. 117.
234. *Ibid.*, p. xi.
235. *Ibid.*, p. xi.
236. *Ibid.*, p. xi.
237. *Ibid.*, p. 2.
238. *Ibid.*, p. 3.
239. *Ibid.*, p. 2.
240. *Ibid.*, p. 9.
241. *Ibid.*, p. 73.
242. *Ibid.*, p. 77.
243. *Ibid.*, p. 132.
244. *Ibid.*, pp. 394-395.

245. *Ibid.*, p. 394.
246. *Ibid.*, p. 153.
247. *Ibid.*, p. 307.
248. *Ibid.*, p. 154, 173.
249. *Ibid.*, p. 195.
250. *Ibid.*, p. 195.
251. *Ibid.*, p. 201
252. *Ibid.*, p. 201.
253. *Ibid.*, p. 207.
254. *Ibid.*, p. 208.
255. *Ibid.*, p. 256.
256. *Ibid.*, p. 256-257.
257. *Ibid.*, p. 257.
258. *Ibid.*, p. 257.
259. *Ibid.*, p. 257.
260. *Ibid.*, p. 255.
261. *Ibid.*, p. 255.
262. *Ibid.*, p. 389.
263. *Ibid.*, p. 259.
264. *Ibid.*, p. 259.
265. *Ibid.*, p. 337.
266. *Ibid.*, p. 320.
267. *Ibid.*, p. 353.
268. *Ibid.*, p. 366.
269. *Ibid.*, p. 373.
270. *Ibid.*, p. 387, 389.
271. *Ibid.*, p. 427.
272. *Ibid.*, p. 427.
273. *Ibid.*, p. 403.
274. *Ibid.*, p. 403.
274. *Ibid.*, p. 430.
276. Jan Anderson and Laurel Hicks, *Introduction to English Literature, Classics for Christians, Vol. 5* (Pensacola, FL: Pensacola Christian College, A Beka Book Publication, 1982).

5

SCIENCE IS BUNK

A senior high school biology textbook attempts to relate all areas of scientific observation and knowledge to the inerrant Word of God. As the author notes at the beginning, "The people who have prepared this book have tried consistently to put the Word of God first and science second."[1] This negative attitude toward science pervades the text. Students are urged to disregard scientific facts and conclusions widely held in the scientific community. "If the conclusions contradict the Word of God, the conclusions are wrong no matter how many scientific facts may appear to back them."[2]

The book looks at various levels of truth, including fallacies, revealed truth and unrevealed truth. Revealed truth includes "those truths which God recorded in Scripture."[3] Unrevealed truths are "those truths, the natural laws, that God established but did not reveal in Scripture."[4] Fallacies include everything else, even if demonstrable scientific evidence suggests that something is true. A fallacy is "that which is contradicted by God's revealed truth, no matter how scientific, how commonly believed, or how apparently workable it may seem. . ."[5] It is also important to remember that "God, according to His timing, permits man to discover scientific knowledge."[6]

118

A negative bias toward science itself appears early on and is linked with the fatalism and acceptance of human imperfectability that corrodes the whole Bob Jones University series of texts. Thus we are told, "There will be sickness, suffering, and death until Christ returns for His thousand-year reign on the earth. Man must now earn his bread by the sweat of his brow because of God's curse upon the earth. The Bible teaches that things are getting worse and that God is the source of all that is good."[7] The scientific method is seen as limited. "It is important for the Christian to realize what science is and the limitations of science so that he can see the proper relationship between science, God, and His Word."[8] Also, "Although some people attribute godlike capabilities to science, science is actually little more than what man can sense around him."[9] In conclusion, "Not only does science have many limitations, but also man is a sinful creature and cannot perfectly rule the earth,"[10] and "It is wrong for a Christian to think that scientific achievements will replace faith in God. . . . science cannot save a man from hell."[11]

The real value in science is this: "True scientific knowledge can enhance your worship by giving you more insight into the wonders of God's creation."[12]

People who are concerned about the environment will wince at this statement, "The first recorded duty of man was a scientific one. In Genesis 1:28 God told man to subdue the earth and to have dominion over it."[13] Little or no concern is shown for the stewardship of creation that many Christians and nonChristians alike see as vital for the preservation of the Earth. Fundamentalists have no interest at all since they see the world on a collision course toward doom. This gloomy negativism is repeated time and again, as in this passage, "Man's power over animals, plants, and even his physical self, however, cannot make him truly good. Only Christ can save him and give him a new heart. No matter how friendly, strong, intelligent, and disease- and disorder-free man is, his righteousness is nothing but filthy rags unless he has a regenerated, cleansed soul."[14]

A major portion of volume one consists of a refutation of the evolutionary process and a defense of Biblical Creationism.[15] The author admits that this is a difficult and dangerous area. "Because Satan has used evolutionary theory effectively against Christians, they should know what they believe concerning this theory."[16]

There are four major points that students must learn from this material: "Creationism and evolution do not mix; The earth is not billions or even millions of years old; Noah's flood is a significant catastrophe, the geological and biological implications of which are usually overlooked; The genetic basis of biological evolution is statistically impossible."[17]

Christians who accept evolution are not true Christians because "One must believe all the Word of God or believe none of it."[18] The text explains further. "A person who believes that God directed evolutionary processes is a theistic evolutionist and is in error. When the Bible states one thing and, in an attempt to be scientific, a person believes something else, he is setting up scientific theory as more authoritative than the Word of God. . . . A person who rejects any portion of the Bible has placed himself above the Bible. The Bible is accurate in *everything*. . ."[19] This philosophical viewpoint affects all of science. "We can be sure that anything that contradicts the Word of God is wrong."[20] This must be held by faith. "Any accurate observation of God's creation could not contradict the revealed Word of God. The Christian's faith can be strengthened by the fact that true science never has contradicted the Bible, and the Christian's faith assures him that it never will."[21]

This text implies that opposition to evolution is not totally based on the concepts of Biblical Creationism. It is to be rejected because believing in evolution relieves "man of his responsibility to God," makes him believe that he "no longer needs a Saviour," and tends toward the "religion of scientism."[22] In addition, "Darwinism is, therefore, contrary to God and His Word in that it blames natural causes for man's present state and hopes in natural causes for man's future."[23]

Finally, evolution is too optimistic for fundamentalist theology. "The great future that man supposedly is pushing toward and that is promised by evolutionary philosophy is not taught in the Bible. Despite scientific advancement, morality and spirituality are declining in our society and will continue to decline."[24]

Still, students are subjected to a chapter "proving" that Darwin and his disciples are wrong. The world, for example, can be no longer than 10,000 years old.[25] In conclusion, students are told: "Biblical creationism is accepted by faith. A creationist, however, should not feel that science contradicts his faith in God's Word. Rather than being disproved by science, the Scriptural concept of a young earth is actually verified by science."[26]

The author continually finds ways to insinuate theology into discussions concerning science. In a discussion on aging and gerontology, we are told, "Christians view aging as a divinely ordained modification of our physical being that came about after the Fall. We should be willing to accept aging, knowing that ultimately we will receive a glorified body that is incorruptible (unaging). Unregenerate people, not having this hope, would like to find some way to block the sequence of aging. . ."[27] In a description of what constitutes death in a clinical sense, we are regaled with this choice passage: "The just, eternal fate of every sinful human being is hell, a place that God prepared for Satan and his hosts. However, Christ also conquered spiritual death so that those who believe on His name would live eternally with Him in their glorified bodies."[28] About diseases we read, "God could have allowed us to live in a disease-free world today in spite of Adam's sin. But He chose to use such afflictions to accomplish His purposes in the lives of men. Many people have come to a saving knowledge of Christ in times of great physical or mental distress because they had nowhere else to turn. . . . God does on occasion use disease as a punishment for sin."[29]

It is difficult to see how any students would respond favorably to the wonders of science after absorbing this volume.

It is doubtful that many would want to pursue careers in this field or to explore further.

The second volume concentrates on zoology, ecology and human reproduction. As expected, every aspect of human and animal anatomy is ascribed to Divine design.   The section on ecology and ecosystems emphasizes human "dominion" over the environment. Environmentalists are seen unfavorably. "To many Christians, the word *ecology* evokes pictures of long-haired protesters carrying signs and marching in front of a nuclear power plant, or it speaks of shelving a project which has already cost taxpayers millions of dollars to save the natural breeding ground of some rare insect."[30]

Furthermore, students are told that "Satan is in control of the physical world around us"[31] and that "Satan has set up this world."[32]

The book delights in ridiculing other social movements, such as animal rights and attempts to limit experimentation on animals.   Animal rights advocates border on pantheism, a "heresy long denounced by Bible-believing Christians."[33] This evil is now being "dressed in new clothes—the New Age movement."[34]   The text says that killing animals to obtain fur or leather "does not violate a Scriptural command."[35] Vegetarians are also ridiculed because "vegetarianism is not advocated in Scripture."[36] In summary, we are told, "In condemning animal abuse, a Christian must be careful not to condemn proper use of what God has given man to use."[37]

Pacifists are also criticized, implicitly. "War is not a desirable event, but in this world it is often necessary."[38]

While some concern for the earth is recommended, it doesn't really matter in the final analysis because this panorama of our future is promised: "The Bible teaches that our world will be destroyed both by what man does to it and by God's destruction. Man's sin is ultimately responsible for the great trumpets of judgment described in Revelation 8 and the vials of God's wrath poured out upon the earth in Revelation 16. These events cause massive destruction of the physical world and the cataclysmic death of most living things."[39]

There is little in modern life that fails to merit condemnation. "Freudian psychology is unreliable and impractical because it leaves out God."[40] Hypnosis is condemned, as is sleeping medicine. "When the still small voice (I Kings 19:11-13) begins to speak to a Christian, teaching him faith by permitting a sorrow in his life, but the Christian takes a pill rather than turning to the Lord, what has he done? When God wants a person to wake up in the night and wrestle with a sin in his life and pray and grow spiritually strong, but he takes another sleeping pill because the last one has worn off, what is he really doing?"[41] Even sleeping too much is deemed sinful. "We can sin by choosing to sleep when we should be doing something else."[42]

The whole attitude expressed toward healing and illness seems medieval or at least premodern. "The Bible teaches us that God controls sickness and health and works His will through both. Sometimes He accomplishes His will through healing, other times through death. . . . If God wants to heal miraculously He will."[43]

Christians are also forbidden to take any medicine that may alter the will or cause psychological dependence, even if prescribed by a physician for a genuine illness. Here is what the text advises: ". . . a Christian who takes psychotropes merely to alter his moods to fit his own wishes is disobeying God. Such a Christian is willfully taking the control of his mind and body away from God. . . . The Christian does not need a psychotrope to help him through life's problems. The unsaved may seek peace of mind and escape from his burdens with a bottle of drugs, but a Christian has a far better source of strength and relief."[44]

When it comes to human sexuality, the text admits no ambiguity, no area of possible disagreement. God "demands sexual purity."[45] Sexual sins are grave sins because "the unsaved will spend their eternity in the torment of hell."[46] This discussion provides a framework for an attack on those who differ, as in this charge to teachers: "Unregenerate psychiatrists may consider adultery and fornication to be normal human behavior in certain situations. Emphasize the dangerous philosophy of situation ethics. Point out the harmful influence of soap operas and other television programs and books that preach the doctrine of sexual freedom."[47] Film and stage personalities are singled out for their allegedly grave transgressions. "Often Hollywood personalities who have been divorced and remarried several times are portrayed as examples of true lovers or ideal marriage partners. Actually, they are failures because they have been selfish and inconsiderate of their spouse's needs. They are merely following their lustful impulses."[48]

About homosexuality we read, "God calls homosexuality a sin, and those who engage in this act are reprobates."[49] Homosexuality is also called "unnatural" in contrast to "normal social relationships."[50] The text does reject the idea that AIDS is a punishment unique to gays, because not all gays have contracted the disease and because some "nonhomosexuals were exposed to the virus in nonsinful ways."[51] However, all sexual sins "are a transgression of God's commandment and defile the body and mind."[52] Therefore, "The diseases that may result are a reminder that God punishes sinners."[53]

Abortion is "the killing of an unborn child."[54] It can never be acceptable. "People may try to redefine the terms and may pass laws to the contrary, but abortion is killing a human—and that is murder."[55] There are no exceptions, even for probable physical deformity. "God has ordained what we call handicapped or deformed. When it comes to deliberately killing a human that we feel is not physically or mental 'normal,' we are ignoring the Bible's teaching about the sovereignty of God and the sanctity of human life."[56] Nothing is said about rape or the possibility of the mother's death.

Euthanasia is also formally condemned.[57]

Evolution receives considerable negative treatment. A U.S. history text says, "Darwin's theory, or modifications of it, have gained wide acceptance, despite the fact that the key premises are unsupported by scientific law or investigation. . . . The main selling point for evolution is not that it has abundant support, but that it explains the universe without referring to God, and so it relieves man of any responsibility to his Creator."[58]

The same text dismisses the Scopes Trial of 1925 as "a mockery of those who believed that the Bible was the Word of God."[59]

An American government textbook gives this assessment of the Scopes Trial. The Scopes Trial is depicted as a terrible assault on true Christians by unbelievers. "Men who preached about the responsibility of man to a holy God and the truth of Scripture soon found themselves scorned by the society around them."[60] Here is the text's portrait of the trial. "While Bryan was a staunch defender of the faith, he did not always handle Darrow's questions well. Bryan was not a Bible scholar or a scientist. Even though Scopes was convicted for teaching evolution, the trial had made Bible-believing Christians appear ignorant and unscientific. The Scopes trial was a disappointment to true Christians, yet they knew that their faith rested in the sure Word of God. Even in such an era of open sin and ridicule of the Bible, some men still stood firm as they preached the truth of Scripture."[61]

Another U.S. history text ridicules Darwin. The discoveries of Charles Darwin are called "pseudo-scientific ideas" which "tore away the moral foundation of the European nations."[62]

The book claims that "Some clear-thinking men in America and Europe began to realize that Darwinism offered a threat to the very existence of true science."[63] President Woodrow Wilson is also cited as a foe of evolution.[64] The motives of those who accepted evolution are frequently questioned. "Creation is contrary to the tenets of materialism, and thus many people, including scientists, had chosen to believe in Darwinism."[65]

An American literature text claims that Darwin's *Origin of Species* brought more attacks against the Word of God than did any other source."[66]

It also expresses a novel view of the Scopes Trial. The case is alleged to have "been set up by a group of outsiders to force their own opinions upon the people of Tennessee."[67] Clarence Darrow is accused of indirectly causing the death of Williams Jennings Bryan. "Throughout the trial Clarence Darrow resorted to emotionalism, name-calling, ridicule, insult, humiliation, and circular reasoning . . . The cruel tactics of Darrow, the ridicule of the press, and the realization that many Americans had fallen for evolution despite his efforts evidently took their toll on William Jennings Bryan; five days after the conclusion of the trial, he died in his sleep."[68]

Other literature texts are suffused with the holy war against evolution. One American literature text includes William Jennings Bryan's "The Bible or Evolution?", which is preceded by this explanation. "Bryan was a fundamental Christian who was influential in bringing about the prohibition of liquor and in preventing the teaching of evolution in the public schools. . . . Bryan won the case against evolution, and the Biblical view of creation was taught in Tennessee for over forty years."[69]

The same textbook includes a sermon on evolution by R. G. Lee, long-time pastor of Bellevue Baptist Church in Memphis, Tennessee. He says, "You can no more believe the Bible and Darwin's theory of evolution than you can be a man and a woman at the same time. . . . Evolution originated in heathenism and ends in atheism. It is violently opposed to the narrative and doctrines of the Bible and destructive of all Christian faith."[70] Evolution "removes that wholesome fear of God so operative in deterring evil and stimulating good."[71] It is both "unscientific and unChristian."[72] Those who accept evolution are "the betrayed dupes of anti-Christ that substitute ethical culture and humanitarianism for regeneration. . ."[73]

Lee concludes with this diatribe: "The statesmen who laid the foundation of the American government made Christianity the chief cornerstone. Today this cornerstone is being undermined by educational institutions that they made possible. The Word of God, in which they put their trust, is now ridiculed by the beneficiaries of their sacrifices."[74]

In still another American literature book, students are told that no Christian may accept the explanation of evolution. "The battle lines between the Bible and evolution were sharply drawn. There was no middle ground, although some—as we shall see later—tried to create one. Darwinism forced people to make a choice between two incompatible explanations for the origin of life."[75]

Scientists themselves are implicitly accused of pride and intellectual arrogance. A British literature text offers this judgment on the scientific community. This text's oft-repeated anti-intellectualism is evident in a passage dealing with the scientific writings of this era. "Most seventeenth-century men of science, unlike so many since, investigated the physical universe with reverence for its Creator. They saw God in nature as well as in the Scriptures and studied 'the book of God's works' as supplementary to the 'Book of God's word.' Unfortunately their achievements, intended as blessings by the divine Source and Revealer of all knowledge, gave occasion to intellectual pride. Regarded as trophies of human genius, these achievements elicited faith in human reason rather than gratitude to God."[76]

Even the Christian scientist Isaac Newton is indirectly criticized. "Newton himself was a devout man and did not intend to encourage ungodliness, but his discoveries made it easier for man to feel that he was in control of his own destiny and no longer needed God."[77]

NOTES

1. William S. Pinkston, Jr., *Biology for Christian Schools, Book 1*, Teacher's Edition (Greenville, SC: Bob Jones University Press, 1991), p. vii.
2. *Ibid.*, p. vii.
3. *Ibid.*, p. 12.
4. *Ibid.*, p. 12.
5. *Ibid.*, p. 12.
6. *Ibid.*, p. 27.
7. *Ibid.*, p. 3.
8. *Ibid.*, p. 25.
9. *Ibid.*, p. 16.
10. *Ibid.*, p. 25.
11. *Ibid.*, p. 28.
12. *Ibid.*, p. 29.
13. *Ibid.*, p. 25.
14. *Ibid.*, p. 169.
15. *Ibid.*, pp. 168-207.
16. *Ibid.*, p. 169.
17. *Ibid.*, p. 169.
18. *Ibid.*, p. 172.
19. *Ibid.*, p. 172.
20. *Ibid.*, p. 173.
21. *Ibid.*, p. 173.
22. *Ibid.*, p. 171.
23. *Ibid.*, p. 197.
24. *Ibid.*, p. 171.
25. *Ibid.*, p. 191.
26. *Ibid.*, p. 191.
27. *Ibid.*, pp. 255-256.
28. *Ibid.*, p. 256.
29. *Ibid.*, p. 245.
30. William S. Pinkston, Jr., *Biology for Christian Schools, Book 2*, Teacher's Edition (Greenville, SC: Bob Jones University Press, 1991), p. 453.

31. *Ibid.*, p. 612.

32. *Ibid.*, p. 647.

33. *Ibid.*, p. 488.

34. *Ibid.*, p. 488.

35. *Ibid.*, p. 489.

36. *Ibid.*, p. 489.

37. *Ibid.*, p. 488.

38. *Ibid.*, p. 491.

39. *Ibid.*, p. 497.

40. *Ibid.*, p. 613.

41. *Ibid.*, p. 625.

42. *Ibid.*, p. 613.

43. *Ibid.*, p. 616.

44. *Ibid.*, p. 626.

45. *Ibid.*, p. 643.

46. *Ibid.*, p. 646.

47. *Ibid.*, p. 645.

48. *Ibid.*, p. 645.

49. *Ibid.*, p. 646.

50. *Ibid.*, p. 647.

51. *Ibid.*, p. 645.

52. *Ibid.*, p. 645.

53. *Ibid.*, p. 645.

54. *Ibid.*, p. 639.

55. *Ibid.*, p. 641.

56. *Ibid.*, p. 640.

57. *Ibid.*, p. 646.

58. Glen Chambers and Gene Fisher, *United States History for Christian Schools* (Greenville, SC: Bob Jones University Press, 1982), p. 330.

59. *Ibid.*, p. 445.

60. Rachel C. Larson with Pamela B. Creason, *The American Republic for Christian Schools* (Greenville, SC: Bob Jones University Press, 1988), p. 496.

61. *Ibid.*, p.496.

62. Michael R. Lowman, *United States History in Christian Perspective* (Pensacola, FL: Pensacola Christian College, A Beka Book Publications, 1983), p. 471.

63. *Ibid.*, p. 508.

64. *Ibid.*, p. 509.

65. *Ibid.*, p. 508.

66. Raymond A. St. John, *American Literature for Christian Schools, Book 1*, (Early American Literature and American Romanticism) Teacher's Edition (Greenville, SC: Bob Jones University Press, 1991), p. 145.

67. *Ibid.*, p. 510.

68. *Ibid.*, pp. 512-513.

69. Jan Anderson and Laurel Hicks, *The Literature of the American People, Classics for Christians, Vol. 4* (Pensacola, FL: Pensacola Christian College, A Beka Book Publications, 1983), p. 268.

70. *Ibid.*, pp. 282, 284.

71. *Ibid.*, p. 287.

72. *Ibid.* p. 286.

73. *Ibid.*, p. 286.

74. *Ibid.*, p. 286.

75. Raymond A. St. John, *American Literature for Christian Schools, Book 2 (Realism, Naturalism, and Modern American Literature)* (Greenville, SC: Bob Jones University Press, 1991), p. 341.

76. Ronald A. Horton, *British Literature for Christian Schools: The Early Tradition, 700-1688* (Greenville, SC: Bob Jones University Press, 1980), p. 299.

77. Chambers and Fisher, p. 82.

6

A POTPOURRI OF

MISCELLANEOUS PREJUDICES

A careful analytical reading of these textbooks reveals a host of prejudices, distortions and novel views of reality not found in comparable educational materials. In this chapter we will examine how the religious presuppositions of the authors affect the selection and interpretation of historical, geographic, and literary material.

AMBIVALENCE TOWARD RELIGIOUS LIBERTY

A considerable reluctance to endorse full religious liberty for all people, and its necessary corollary, the separation of church and state, is a prominent characteristic of an eleventh-grade American history text.

The considerable admiration shown for the Puritans and Pilgrims and for those colonies which restricted worship to established churches or to multiple establishment of Protestants is one clue to the textual bias.

In its portrait of Roger Williams' Rhode Island colony, the text says, "Although the separation of church and state is a

valid principle, the fact that it was carried to extremes in Rhode
Island encouraged many religious malcontents to settle there."[1]

Anne Hutchinson's banishment from Massachusetts Bay
Colony is at least implicitly supported because "much of her
teaching opposed both Puritan beliefs and the Bible."[2] Also,
she allegedly taught that "the Bible was not God's final revelation."[3] She seems to have gotten her just desserts though. "She
continued to preach her radical beliefs in New York until she
was killed in her home by Indians in 1643."[4] It is also significant that the hanging of Mary Dyer, a Quaker, is omitted from
this history. So is any reference to Catholics who suffered
martyrdom.

Only minorities seem to benefit from religious freedom.
"The Catholics in Maryland, the Anglicans in Massachusetts, and
the Presbyterians and Baptists in all the colonies wanted religious
liberty because they were minority groups. The unchurched
minority wanted liberty from all religions and contributed to the
eventual separation of church and state, but the unchurched by
themselves could neither have founded nor have maintained a
free republic. True republican governments cannot survive
without moral citizens, and most of the unchurched wanted
freedom from moral restraints."[5]

This grudging acceptance of religious liberty shows up
again in this comment about the adoption of the Federal Bill of
Rights. "Christians from states whose constitutions acknowledged the superiority of God's Law and the need for His
blessings failed to understand why the national Constitution could
not have done the same."[6] The authors also devote no attention
to the ban on religious tests for public office contained in Article
VI.

In another passage the text claims that God inspired
God's men to write the Constitution. "Because they were
products of a society that maintained a strong biblical emphasis,
they accepted the biblical view of man and government. This
view caused them to agree that human nature is corrupt, that
human government is inferior to a higher law, and that society

should be orderly."[7]   However, in a splendid example of authorial judgmentalism, we are informed, "This does not mean that all the Founding Fathers were Christians. Many were not. Some were evasive about their religious beliefs, and a few, like Benjamin Franklin, frankly denied the fundamentals of the Christian faith. None of the delegates to the convention were atheists, however; all were men of Christian principle, products of Puritanism, who accepted biblical principles, to at least some degree, as the basis for human law."[8]

Students are also informed that the Founders gave only "what God wanted for His people, not necessarily what the citizens wanted for themselves."[9]

This limited view of human liberty is seen in another passage in which the nation's early settlers are said to believe that "liberty was not a natural right, but a God-given right, restricted by God's authority as revealed in the Bible. The Reformation had prepared them for the task of establishing God-honoring societies. Step by step, year by year, these societies grew in the new land."[10]

This view of liberty is related to a concept of America that presupposes that the Hand of God directed its affairs, a view widely held among nineteenth century evangelicals and one that is still held by those who write these texts.

At the very beginning of this history text, students are told, "The United States is a special nation. . . because it, more than any other nation in modern history, has been founded and built upon biblical principles. Consequently, it has been unusually blessed by God."[11] Throughout the book, this claim is reiterated repeatedly and is related to a belief in American exceptionalism. "Those who founded the American colonies were, for the most part, deeply religious. Not all of them were Christians in the biblical sense of the term, but they all recognized God as the Creator and Ruler of the earth. No other nation has been grounded so thoroughly in religious belief and biblical truth. It is no accident that this nation eventually became the strongest and most prosperous on earth."[12]

About the drafting of the Constitution, we are told, "The hand of God was obvious in the adoption, ratification, and support of the Constitution. . . . All the events preceding the Constitution had led the colonies and states farther apart. As God directed, they were brought together for the first time. This unity was accomplished only as the direct result of the providence and power of a gracious, loving God."[13]

It is also interesting to learn that "The Louisiana Purchase resulted more from God's providence than from Jefferson's ingenuity."[14]   After the War of 1812, "God preserved the American people and nation for further service."[15]   It is asserted that even though the Civil War was terrible, "God graciously preserved this nation, through no merit of its own, for His own reasons."[16]   Finally, "America's biblical background made a difference in the years following the Civil War."[17]

THREE CHEERS FOR THE PURITANS

Closely allied to a sentimental reverencing of idealized pasts is the fondness for Puritan ways, shown repeatedly in literature and history texts. A decided dislike for immigrants is related to this fondness for Anglo-Saxon Puritanism. Here is how a civics text presents these sensitive issues.

"America had received a godly heritage from its early Pilgrim and Puritan fathers. Even through the 1700s and early 1800s, most of the people who had come to America were from a Protestant background. While many were not true Christians, most of these earlier Americans had a respect for the Bible as the Word of God and a belief in its moral standards. The immigration of the 1800s and the changes in American society, however, greatly altered the nation's religious attitudes.[18] "The influence of non-Protestant immigrants and immigrants with rationalist and other liberal views led to more rejection of the inerrancy of the Bible, a greater acceptance of the social gospel, and an increased decay of Christian character in the nation."[19]

In other words, America would have been a better nation if only Protestants had been allowed to settle here.

Strange comments abound. "Some immigrant groups were particularly heavy drinkers, and their actions were offensive to many others."[20] One assumes that native-born Americans never allowed demon rum to pass their lips. In a discussion of Scandinavian immigrants we are told, "Most were Lutheran and had come to America in protest of the policies of their churches back home."[21] If this were true, why have the majority of Scandinavian immigrants and their ancestors remained Lutheran?

A widely-used history text portrays the Puritans in an entirely favorable light. "Like the Pilgrims, the Puritans came to America to fulfill a God-given mission of establishing churches that practiced scriptural teachings. . . . the Puritans were given a unique opportunity: they were able to establish a civil society that was governed by Bible-believing Christians. . . .the Puritans soon earned the reputation of being diligent, thrifty, and honest."[22] Even their banishments of dissenters are justified. "The Puritan banishments were harsh, but from the Puritan viewpoint they were completely justified. The Puritans had made it clear what they believed and what they wanted to accomplish in the New World—the establishment of communities that were based on scriptural beliefs. . . . Those who disagree with Puritan doctrine must still admire their sincerity and consistency; despite their flaws, they deserve respect."[23]

Puritan repression is acceptable. "Puritan society established strict rules to help the citizens keep their old natures reined in. One reason that modern society views the Puritans as odd is that modern society has departed from the Word of God, by which the Puritans ordered their lives."[24] In summary, "Nonetheless, Puritanism produced a way of life that emphasized morality and respected the Bible. The benefits of Puritanism to our nation far outweigh its failures."[25]

Even the Salem witch trials are whitewashed. "Since the Bible clearly teaches that witchcraft is real and since the Puritans had witnessed what they were certain were instances of witch-craft among the Indians, they were simply afraid. Like many other horrible events in history, the Salem witchcraft trials were mostly the result of fear. . . .They were not at all typical of colonial America in general or of Puritanism in particular."[26]

REVIVALISM

These texts wax eloquent in their discussions of religious revivals and their alleged impact on U.S. history. Revivals form a major part of the Chambers-Fisher text. The text repeatedly emphasizes revivalism as a positive and influential factor in U.S. history. Four full pages are devoted to the "Great Awakening" of the 1740s, which "is a particularly clear example of the Holy Spirit's use of a few surrendered men to accomplish great things in the lives of a great many people."[27] These revivals "were characterized by powerful preaching, effectual prayer meetings, and diligent personal witnessing by church members. As a result many were converted, and there was both a significant increase in church membership and a renewed vigor among church members."[28]

The Great Awakening is said to have produced several other favorable events. It "promoted religious liberty, because it had been independent of established churches. . . . it checked the spread of heresy that was beginning to invade the colonies. . . it promoted a spirit of unity among the evangelical groups throughout the colonies."[29]

Finally, "God used the Great Awakening to cause a revitalization of biblical Christianity in the colonies. Revived faith would help prepare the colonists to survive two wars and to found a new nation."[30]

Four and a half pages of text are devoted to something called "The Great Revival" of the late 1790s and early 1800s in Kentucky, Pennsylvania and other states. The text states that the revivals helped to preserve America and enabled the new nation to survive the War of 1812. "To credit the survival of the fledgling republic wholly to the Constitution and political leadership is hardly realistic. Indeed, many Christians believed that America would have died in its early decades, despite its Constitution and its statesmen, had it not been for another very important influence. Just when it was most needed, a great revival resurrected the national morality that had been lost during and after the war with England. National morality was essential to America's existence; a free nation cannot continue to exist without a self-governed, moral people. And nothing produces morality so well as a general acceptance of biblical standards."[31]

After claiming that "In 1799 many of the people in the western part of the middle and southern states were unchurched and unconcerned about spiritual matters. . . . In the summer of 1801, a meeting at Cane Ridge in Bourbon county, Kentucky, began to change the character of the West. . . . This genuine conviction resulted in the transformation of many families and communities."[32]

Hailing the Methodist, Presbyterian and Baptist meetings, the authors claim that "hundreds went home assured of their personal salvation and burdened that friends and relatives also be converted. The effects spread rapidly. . . . Even Dan Morgan, the war hero, may have been converted at a revival in western Virginia after his retirement. As individual lives were transformed, there was a noticeable change in the morality of the West."[33]

Revivalism's impact on colleges is discussed. "After the war, colleges that had been founded specifically for the training of Christian leaders were producing students who were essentially atheists. The acceptance of French infidelity was more or less general in all the major colleges. . . . Of the major Christian colleges, only Harvard was relatively untouched by the Great Revival. It became more solidly entrenched in infidelity."[34] Changes at Yale are described. "Student behavior at Yale before the revival was similar to that in other colleges. Idleness, gambling, and drinking had become serious problems. Even more serious was the students' growing rejection of the Bible. Doubts that the Bible was the Word of God were openly expressed by most of the students during the presidency of Ezra Stiles. . . . Within just a few years, virtually every student at Yale recognized biblical truth. . . .Yale remained spiritually responsive for at least two decades."[35]   Therefore, "The nation's generally biblical morality, encouraged by the Great Revival, increased the national spiritual quality. As a result, the people were generally law-abiding. . . ."[36]

Linked to this was the development of Sunday Schools. "Christians especially believed that God had special plans for the United States and that the fulfillment of those plans required a godly people. One result of this conviction was the formation of Sunday schools."[37] Even here, slurs toward other faiths are introduced. "In 1817 the American Sunday School Union was formed in Philadelphia. Of the three men most instrumental in its founding, one was a Universalist, who did not believe in the deity of Christ; one was a Roman Catholic; and the third was a Protestant Episcopal [sic]. From its inception the association emphasized morality more than the gospel, and it became more liberal as time progressed."[38]

Nearly a page of text is devoted to Adoniram Judson, an American Baptist missionary to Burma, and to the "Haystack" Prayer Meeting of 1806.

This posture is reiterated in a section on the Finney revivals of the 1820s. "The Great Revival had contributed to improving the moral and spiritual quality of the people as a whole, and the nation was reaping the benefits. Adding to the effect of that revival were the results of the Finney revivals. . . . Finney's revivals reached their peak during Jackson's administration. Probably as many as 500,000 were converted as a direct result of his meetings."[39]   An unusual interpretive twist is added, however. "The Finney revivals and others of the time, in contrast to the Great Awakening of the 1740s, emphasized the love of God more than His holiness. They also tended to emphasize humanitarian endeavors more than the study of the Bible."[40]

The "Prayer Meeting Revival" of the 1850s is given prominence. "God used the political, economic, and emotional turmoil of the 1850s to turn many Americans to Himself. . . . Perhaps half a million people were saved as a direct result, and the spiritual quality of the United States was revived, especially in the Northeast."[41] The text can't resist another slur. "Noon prayer meetings also began in Boston, despite Unitarian opposition."[42]

A major section is devoted to revivals in the Confederate Army during the Civil War. "Throughout the Civil War there were continuing revivals in the Confederate army. . . . Revivals came largely because several officers were burdened for the spiritual welfare of their men."[43]

General Stonewall Jackson is described as a "Presbyterian deacon" whose "primary interests were spiritual."[44] General Robert E. Lee is also praised. "Lee faithfully attended prayer and preaching services and frequently encouraged his soldiers to do the same."[45] Significantly, however, Lee's lifelong adherence to the Episcopal Church is omitted, continuing the anti-Episcopalian bias of the authors. Note that Jackson's Presbyterianism was mentioned.

The alleged results are described. "Because of the influence of Lee, Jackson, and other Christian officers, many Confederate soldiers were converted. Numerous Bible-preaching churches were then established in the South following the war, and to this day the Old South is referred to as the 'Bible belt.'"[46] This is inaccurate since "the Bible Belt" also refers to major portions of the rural North and West, where evangelical religion is pervasive. The Old South, in fact, is substantially Catholic or Episcopalian, particularly in the coastal regions.

Nearly one page is devoted to a sympathetic portrait of the Dwight L. Moody revivals of the late nineteenth century.[47]

Finally, baseball player turned evangelist Billy Sunday is given nearly a page of praise. "Over a million hearers 'hit the

sawdust trail' and found Christ as their Savior."[48] His Presbyterian identification and opposition to the "liquor industry" are
noted.

This excessive if not inordinate attention to revivalism is
questionable.   Many historians see the revivals as *internal*
aspects of conservative Protestantism, a method of church
growth unique to this religious community, not as far-reaching
events in the nation's total history. Since they were (and are)
essentially internal events intrinsic to one community, a case
could be made that events central to other religious traditions,
such as social reform, confessionalism, the neo-Gothic movement in church architecture and liturgy, or ecumenism could also
be mentioned in a U.S. history course.

Revivalism also had its dark side. It was a divisive social
movement, which led to disdain and prejudice toward other
Christian traditions which emphasized reason rather than
emotion, traditional liturgy and worship, and an intellectual
approach to religious questions. None of the complexities of
revivalism are ever touched upon in the wholly laudatory pages
of material devoted to the subject.   A world history text[49] also
spends six pages praising the pietists and revivalists of eighteenth
century England and Germany. An American history text makes
claims for evangelism's impact on U.S. society that are not
accepted by most scholars. Of evangelist Billy Sunday it is said:
"When he preached to thousands in a city, the tone of the whole
city was changed.   Thieves with new hearts became honest
working men, and formerly dishonest politicians became
crusaders for public decency. Because of Billy Sunday and the
power of the gospel, many cities in America became morally
cleaner, safer, and more pleasant places in which to live.
Because of his hard preaching against liquor, particularly his
famous 'booze' sermon, many saloons closed down for lack of
business."[50]

TREATMENT OF RACIAL MINORITIES

In all of these texts, black Americans are referred to as Negroes. The treatment accorded them is ambivalent. In Chambers and Fisher their achievements are rarely noted. Booker T. Washington[51] and George Washington Carver[52] are praised for their "moderation," but about W.E.B. DuBois it is said, "In 1926 and 1936 he visited the Soviet Union. He became a loud and devoted socialist; late in life he joined the Communist party and eventually renounced his American citizenship."[53]

The treatment of Dr. Martin Luther King, Jr. is far from friendly. "Because he couched his speeches in peaceful terminology, he gained a reputation as a man of peace; he was even awarded the Nobel Peace Prize in 1964. . . .King had become a symbol of civil rights; his death brought violence and destruction in several parts of the country. Like Kennedy, he was viewed by many as a martyr for human rights; his increasing shift to the left, especially in the last year of his life, was soon forgotten."[54]

The Civil Rights movement of the 1960s is dismissed this way. "Encouraged by Kennedy's promise of support, Negroes began demanding equal social rights. . . . During Kennedy's administration civil rights leaders made steps toward gaining better treatment for Negroes, but the demonstrations increased hatred and bitterness among many. . . . As violence increased, the leadership of civil rights organizations became more militant."[55]

Even the section on slavery is not as forthright as one would expect. The students are told that "the Bible does not specifically condemn slavery . . . It is clear that the problem of slavery was not a simple one. . . . The story of slavery in America is an excellent example of the far-reaching consequences of sin. The sin in this case was greed . . ."[56] While slavery is seen as harsh, slaves were not always blameless. "He sometimes expressed his unwillingness, despite whippings and other harsh treatment, by destroying crops, working slowly, or running away."[57]   It is also claimed, "Even most free Negroes in the North were illiterate, and public sentiment in both the North and the South opposed educating them."[58]

We are also told that "The Negro vote had placed Grant in office."[59] Finally, "American Christians in particular might have done more to help the Negro become all that he could, intellectually, morally, and spiritually."[60]

This generally unfavorable treatment of African-Americans is a noteworthy characteristic of this text.

As we have also seen, the civil rights movement of the 1960s through the present is unfavorably depicted.

NATIVE AMERICANS

Native Americans are always referred to as Indians. Neither their culture nor religion is treated with respect. Indian culture is disparaged. "The concept of sin was foreign to the Indian culture; discipline was intended to teach children to survive rather than to make them moral. This amoral philosophy was often discouraging to Christian missionaries, who found it difficult to teach Indians the difference between right and wrong. . . . The Indian culture typified heathen civilization—lost in darkness without the light of the gospel."[61]

However, "some Indians came to accept Christ as Saviour,"[62] due to the efforts of Protestant missionaries. Nothing is said about the much more numerous successes by Catholic missionaries.

One Native American tribe, the Cherokee, is admired. Apparently there are good Indians and bad Indians, the good ones being those who converted to Protestantism. "The Cherokees were particularly receptive to the white man's customs. They expressed a yearning to know more about the white man's God and His Book. Mission work among these Indians was especially successful."[63] A Cherokee letter to Congress from 1822 is quoted. It says, in part, "The exertions and labors of various religious societies in these United States are successfully engaged in promulgating to them the words of truth and life from the sacred volume of Holy Writ. . ."[64] The text continues, "Similar claims by most other Indian tribes would have been dishonest . . . Mission schools flourished; many Cherokees lived consistent Christian lives."[65]

Here is the commentary on the Sioux Wars. "The more warlike tribes hindered railroad building, stampeded cattle, wiped out wagon trains, destroyed telegraph lines, and burned settlers' property. Their resistance proved useless, however, as increasing numbers of settlers, aided by troops, repeatedly defeated them. By the 1880s most had given up and were confined to reservations."[66] The Battle of Wounded Knee on December 29, 1890 is given a rather complicated explanation, suggesting that it was all a mistake and that the Indians were massacred "despite efforts by cavalry officers to prevent it."[67]

Native Americans are viewed with disdain in another text, as in this passage, "The Indians who terrorized the miners and cowboys terrorized the settlers too. Disgruntled over the loss of their lands and the destruction of the buffalo, the Indians were quick to go on the rampage."[68]

Here is how Native Americans are presented in a middle-school level text. "These Indians lived in a very wild fashion. They spent much of their time in hunting, fishing, and fighting. . . . People say that they were badly treated by the European settlers, but they treated one another worse than the settlers ever did."[69]

Another passage says, "The Dutch in New York also had their troubles with the Indians. They paid for all the lands they took, but one of their governors was foolish enough to start a war that went on for two years. Worse trouble started in North Carolina, where there was a powerful tribe called the Tuscaroras. These warriors attacked the settlers and murdered numbers of them. But in the end they were driven out of that part of the country."[70]

ANTI-INTELLECTUALISM

In subtle and not-so-subtle ways, students are warned against pursuing the life of the mind. They are constantly told that the intellectual leaders of society, the writers and scientists especially, are often in the forefront of apostate movements that challenge or deny the Gospel. Even clergy are more likely to betray the faith than the simple-minded laity. Secular colleges and universities are portrayed as centers of apostasy, as in this reference from Chambers and Fisher, "Because colleges tend to exalt knowledge and reason above faith, they are often the first social institution to experience religious decline."[71]

A world history volume says that "many scientists and philosophers of the Enlightenment put their faith in reason instead of God's revelation, the Bible."[72] The same text affirms that many modern people "looked to the social theories of intellectuals who promised a perfect society while others trusted in the cult of science. Some religious leaders and theologians departed from the 'old-time religion.'"[73]

A modern American literature text claims that "leading American thinkers, rejecting the Bible view of man, regarded man as merely an animal or reverenced him as God."[74] This text is also blunt in another passage: "Professional religionists are often the least informed and, in fact, may be themselves conscious deceivers."[75]

NOSTALGIA FOR THE GOOD OLD DAYS

A decided preference for earlier, and presumably more moral, times is conveyed by these texts. All prefer the Puritan and colonial days in America, when the dominant patterns of culture were set by "Bible-believing" churches and virtually everyone in positions of authority was white, Protestant, and male. (Victorian England is also hailed as the Golden Age for that country.)

Americans were more pure, holy, and likely to believe the Bible as infallible during those days. The schools reflected those values. Teachers were all Christians. The Bible and pious literature were read. Society was nicer and safer.

This nostalgic longing for the past is revealed in several ways. In a Pensacola Christian College publication for American history students, a decided preference is shown for an idealized past when American life was pure and virtuous. "A reverence for God permeated American culture" in the nineteenth century,[76] we are informed. The text also claims that "eleven out of twelve high school graduates" attended private or church-related schools before 1890.[77] The nineteenth century is also described in these ways: ". . . the broad truths of the Bible permeated American society and set the cultural and moral tone of the country. . . . The Bible continued to be the nation's most honored book. . . . Most of the churches continued to respect the Bible as the inspired Word of God."[78]

Public schools were also safe bastions of Christianity in those wonderful days. "Parents could send their children to school knowing that the values they taught their children at home would be reinforced in the public school. Many of the public school teachers were Christians, and nearly all of them honored the Bible. The schools were run by the communities, which were composed of people who honored God's Word. Bible reading and prayer were part of the daily routine in each school."[79]

An American government book shows a clear preference for colonial America and its pattern of religious freedom and education. "Colonial Christians were much more conscious of God's working than most Christians today."[80] We are also told that "God has shaped the history of America" because of "its founding by English colonists, its strong Protestant background, and a government and Constitution recognizing moral and Biblical principles."[81]

An American literature text has this to say about an earlier America. "Despite two world wars and the Great

Depression, a majority of Americans during the first half of the century believed the Bible and had faith in God. Almost half of the people in the early part of the century were church members, and most churches were true to the Bible. Liquor was outlawed in many areas, and a high standard of morality was generally upheld by the majority of the people."[82]

PROHIBITION

Several texts argue that Prohibition was a noble venture favored by all Christians. It was eventually repealed, they say, only because of the obstinacy and inherent corruption of the American people and the failure of law enforcement officials to enforce it.

Prohibition is hailed as a noble attempt to reform society even though human sinfulness and ineffective law enforcement doomed it to failure. "Prohibition did bring some benefits. Less alcohol was consumed, and some people gave up drinking. There was less gambling. Alcohol-related diseases and deaths decreased, and sober workers were more efficient. When prohibition was repealed, liquor freely began to afflict Americans with its sad effects again."[83]

Prohibition of alcoholic beverages by law is said to have had more "widespread popularity than any other amendment to the U.S. Constitution," [84] which is patently absurd. A rural-dominated political system in Congress and the state legislatures is largely responsible for passage of the Eighteenth Amendment. Statewide prohibition attempts were often defeated, as in conservative, largely Protestant Iowa in 1917. Still, this book claims that "Christians" supported it and that it "brought many benefits to the nation."[85] As a matter of historical fact, only Anglo-Saxon evangelical Protestants and some Scandinavian pietists were solidly in favor of national Prohibition. Catholics, Jews, Unitarians, Episcopalians, Lutherans and religious liberals were opposed to its passage. The campaign for Prohibition was one of the most sectarian and divisive in the nation's history. If anything, a religious minority imposed its will on an unwilling nation, and rampant lawlessness and corruption resulted.

Students reading this book receive a completely different view of history. The text claims that Prohibition failed only because an insufficient number of agents were involved in the effort, and many of them were "inept or unethical."[86] Also, "much harm was done by the failure of citizens to cooperate with the prohibition law."[87] After repeal these were the fruits: "the number of alcoholics reached alarming heights, and there were rapid increases in drug addiction, psychiatric cases, divorce rates, and the instability of the family."[88] It is altogether a simplistic interpretation of history.[89]

IMPERIALISM

One of the most controversial ideas advanced is the contention that Western imperialism was admirable because it led to expansion of Protestant missions in Third World countries. Imperialism "illustrates how God uses natural means to accomplish His divine purpose. For the most part, imperialism was initiated by ungodly men and for ungodly motives. Yet God used 'the wrath of man' for His praise: imperialism was a means by which the gospel was spread to the far corners of the globe."[90] In addition, it is solemnly affirmed that "Christian missionaries were not motivated by a desire to exploit or subject foreign peoples."[91] This is contrary to the historical record in many lands. The close ties between missions and their nations led to considerable church-state conflict. In Africa it has been a factor in the rise of indigenous Christian churches. Also, not a word is devoted to Catholic missions, which were at least as successful in penetrating non-European cultures and in shaping the historical development of those lands.

President William McKinley's justification of U. S. intervention in the Philippines is praised because it "sums up the positive side of western imperialism."[92] McKinley told Congress that one of his goals in the U.S. takeover of the Philippines was to "uplift and civilize and Christianize them."[93]

APOCALYPTICISM

A widely-used American history text asserts uncompromisingly the fundamentalist-prophetic view of modern Middle East politics. "The Middle East has remained the critical area of the world not only because of its vast oil resources, but also because Israel is the focal point of God's plan for the last days. As the return of Christ draws nearer, the world's attention will be on Palestine."[94]

WE'RE SURROUNDED

These texts convey a siege mentality to students and reinforce the desire for separateness and nonengagement with the larger culture—except in efforts to convert the heathen majority. True Christians, students are repeatedly told, are a small minority, certain to be misunderstood and persecuted. All other religious groups are evil and threatening and must be held at bay. Virtually every new idea or trend in government, science, literature, or social relationships must be resisted. Hostility toward modernity in all areas is encouraged.

This negative attitude toward modern life and ideas can only predispose students to rightwing social and political forces which seek to return to some romanticized past, when a more acceptable lifestyle was allegedly preserved. This is not status-quo affirming conservatism; it is hard-right reaction, a decided preference for an earlier America dominated by evangelical churches and paternalistic capitalism.

Moreover, students are constantly warned and cajoled to accept their persecution as the lot of the elect, of those who have found favor with God—while the vast majority of humanity heads for eternal damnation.

Anyone daring or foolhardy enough to question these text's religious assertions receives an immediate put-down. "Of course, believing the Bible to be wholly God's Word requires faith, and thus the unsaved man, lacking faith, will naturally attempt to deny the truth of the Bible, because it reveals his sin."[95] For example, those secular historians who believe the Great Awakening's influence on history has been exaggerated receive this stern judgment. "Enemies of the Great Awakening, then and since, have attacked preachers such as Edwards and Whitefield because they preached the Scriptures plainly and emphasized the truths of the gospel. We should not forget that unsaved men who are not spiritually discerning usually fail to grasp spiritual truths."[96]

NOTES

1. Glen Chambers and Gene Fisher, *United States History for Christian Schools* (Greenville, SC: Bob Jones University Press, 1982), p. 43.
2. *Ibid.*, p. 43.
3. *Ibid.*, p. 43.
4. *Ibid.*, p. 43.
5. *Ibid.*, p. 55.
6. *Ibid.*, p. 205.
7. *Ibid.*, p. 162.
8. *Ibid.*, pp. 162-63.
9. *Ibid.*, p. 163.
10. *Ibid.*, p. 35.
11. *Ibid.*, p. 11.
12. *Ibid.*, p. 86.
13. *Ibid.*, p. 176.
14. *Ibid.*, p. 191.
15. *Ibid.*, p. 197.
16. *Ibid.*, p. 323.
17. *Ibid.*, p. 311.

18. Rachel C. Larson with Pamela B. Creason, *The American Republic for Christian Schools* Greenville, SC: Bob Jones University Press, 1988), pp. 445-446.

19. *Ibid.*, p. 106T.

20. *Ibid.*, p. 447.

21. *Ibid.*, p. 382.

22. Chambers and Fisher, p. 41.

23. *Ibid.*, p. 44.

24. *Ibid.*, p. 57.

25. *Ibid.*, p. 71.

26. *Ibid.*, p. 82.

27. *Ibid.*, p. 83.

28. *Ibid.*, p. 83.

29. *Ibid.*, p. 86.

30. *Ibid.*, p. 86.

31. *Ibid.*, p. 197.

32. *Ibid.*, p. 198.

33. *Ibid.*, p. 198.

34. *Ibid.*, pp. 199, 200.

35. *Ibid.*, pp. 200, 201.

36. *Ibid.*, p. 201.

37. *Ibid.*, p. 200.

38. *Ibid.*, p. 200.

39. *Ibid.*, p. 235.

40. *Ibid.*, p. 239.

41. *Ibid.*, p. 279.

42. *Ibid.*, p. 279.

43. *Ibid.*, p. 301.

44. *Ibid.*, p. 301.

45. *Ibid.*, p. 301.

46. *Ibid.*, p. 301.

47. *Ibid.*, p. 326.

48. *Ibid.*, p. 412.

49. David A. Fisher, *World History for Christian Schools* (Greenville, SC: Bob Jones University Press, 1984).

50. Michael R. Lowman, *United States History in Christian Perspective* (Pensacola, FL: Pensacola Christian College, A Beka Book Publication, 1983), p. 518.

51. Chambers and Fisher, pp. 335-337.

52. *Ibid.*, p. 441.

53. *Ibid.*, p. 445.

54. *Ibid.*, pp. 564, 574-75.

55. *Ibid.*, pp. 563, 565, 574.

56. *Ibid.*, pp. 236, 237.

57. *Ibid.*, p. 237.

58. *Ibid.*, p. 335.

59. *Ibid.*, p. 317.

60. *Ibid.*, p. 318.

61. *Ibid.*, pp. 76-77.

62. *Ibid.*, p. 77.

63. *Ibid.*, p. 240.

64. *Ibid.*, p. 241.

65. *Ibid.*, p. 241.

66. *Ibid.*, p. 352.

67. *Ibid.*, p. 369.

68. Larson and Creason, p. 420.

69. Michael J. McHugh and Charles Morris, *A Child's Story of America* (Arlington Heights, IL: Christian Liberty Press, 1989), p. 64.

70. *Ibid.*, p. 70.

71. Chambers and Fisher, p. 80.

72. Fisher, p. 386.

73. *Ibid.*, p. 486.

74. Raymond A. St. John, *American Literature for Christian Schools, Book 2, (Realism, Naturalism, and Modern American Literature*) Teacher's Edition (Greenville, SC: Bob Jones University Press, 1991), p. 537.

75. *Ibid.*, p. 616.

76. Lowman, p. 232.

77. *Ibid.*, p. 383.

78. *Ibid.*, p. 386.

79. *Ibid.*, p. 387.

80. Larson and Creason, p. 53.

81. *Ibid.*, p. 141T.

82. Jan Anderson and Laurel Hicks, *Classics for Christians, Vol. 4* (Pensacola, FL: Pensacola Christian College, A Beka Book Publication, 1983), p. 252.

83. Larson and Creason, p. 495.

84. Lowman, p. 520.

85. *Ibid.*, p. 520.

86. *Ibid.*, p. 520.

87. *Ibid.*, p. 520.

88. *Ibid.*, p. 520.

89. For an extensive discussion of the religious elements in the Prohibition movement see *Pressure Politics*, by Peter H. Odegard (New York: Columbia University Press, 1928), and *Prohibition in Kansas*, by Robert Smith Bader (Lawrence, KS: University Press of Kansas, 1986).

90. Fisher, p. 499.

91. *Ibid.*, p. 499.

92. *Ibid.*, p. 512.

93. *Ibid.*, p. 512.

94. Chambers and Fisher, p. 577.

95. Larson and Creason, p. 45T.

96. *Ibid.*, p. 59.